DANCING WITH THE ENERGY OF CONFLICT AND TRAUMA

Letting Go, Finding Peace
In Families, Communities, & Nations

DR. MARK UMBREIT

Contents

THE ENERGY OF BEING REAL

Mark Nepo
The Book of Awakening

"Mana" is a term originally used in Polynesian and Melanesian cultures to describe an extraordinary power or force residing in a person or an object, a sort of spiritual electricity that charges anyone who touches it.

Without any intent to shape others, we simply have to be authentic, and a sense of spiritual light and warmth will emanate from our very souls, causing others to grow- not toward us, but toward the light that moves through us. In this way, by being who we are, we not only experience life in all its vitality, but, quite innocently and without design, we help others be more thoroughly themselves. In being real, in staying devoted to this energy of realness, we help each other grow toward the one vital light.

Acknowledgements

The creation of this book is grounded in the stories of many courageous individuals who found the inner strength to let go of the emotional entrapment that traumatic events and severe conflicts so often entail. In doing so, they found varying degrees of inner peace, serenity, and freedom. I want to first acknowledge these individuals.

The editorial support and guidance provided by my friends Ted Lewis, Marilyn Armour, and Bill Bradshaw was deeply appreciated. Their contributions were numerous, more than they probably realize. Thank you Ted, Marilyn, and Bill.

My student assistant Joel Grostephan provided helpful assistance with research and early drafts of the manuscript. His background as a journalist proved to be very helpful.

Special recognition is due to Kerry Voight. As I was near completion of the manuscript, I had a life threatening accident that disabled me for an extended period of time. With her background and talent as a creative writer, Kerry provided enormous assistance in the final preparation and formatting of the book. Without her talent and energy, this book would not have been finalized in a timely manner.

Special recognition is also due to Jennifer Blevins, my doctoral Research Assistant. Her editorial skills and support were vital to the final completion of the book.

Finally, I want to acknowledge the most important people in my life that represent the core of my capacity to do the work I have been engaged in over the past four decades, to mediate, to facilitate, to teach, to write, to conduct research, and most importantly, to dance with the energy of conflict and trauma in my own life and to witness the dance of so many others. The unconditional love and support of my life partner of more than four decades, as well as the joy and playfulness of our daughters, their husbands, and our grandkids has been and will always remain the anchor of my being, the source of my energy, and the grounding of my life work, infusing it with perspective, humility, balance, playfulness, and serenity. Thank you Lex, Jenni, Terrill, Myles, Jade, Laura, Enrico, and Sophie for your loving presence in my life.

PRAISE FOR DANCING WITH THE ENERGY OF CONFLICT AND TRAUMA

During these challenging times of anger, intolerance and conflict, Mark Umbreit brings us an important book, which through his own storytelling teaches us how to deeply listen to each other and to grow as a community of humans caring for one another. This much needed book captures Professor Umbreit's remarkable work in restorative justice through his sensitive cross cultural work by bringing warmth, understanding, collaboration and dialogue in working with the energy of all parties. Mark has contributed in so many ways to the development of restorative justice in the United States and around the world. *Dancing With the Energy of Conflict and Trauma* is a gift to all, as Mark shares his own personal journey through life, conflict and growth.

> Janine P. Geske (retired WI Supreme Court Justice), Distinguished Professor of Law and Director of the Marquette University Law School Restorative Justice Initiative

Dr. Umbreit writes with passion about the role of energy in conflict, trauma, and healing. His book is a must read for everyone who cares about building and preserving a peaceful coexistence with others and with the self at a very deep level. This book is not just for those of us who have been cracked wide open, crushed at times by despair, or whose souls have been cannibalized by the ugly grip of deep, dark, sorrows and pain that ensue after experiencing traumas such as war, torture, rape, life threatening illness, or losses and betrayals of all kinds and levels; though it will enlighten and give valuable tools to those who are on the journey of healing from the multifaceted marks of trauma. Neither is it just for those in the caring professions that are trying to make sense of, and help others heal from conflict and trauma. It is for anyone that wants to gain a deeper understanding of the true compass of self, and practice mindful interdependence with nature and others. *Dancing with the Energy of Conflict and Trauma* is a tool kit to understand and decode the language of the soul, Energy!

Kifah Abdi, Survivor of Torture

Each of us will experience the woundedness that comes from conflict or traumatic events at some point in our lives. In *Dancing with the Energy of Conflict and Trauma,* Mark Umbreit shares deeply touching stories of transformation where those on both sides of conflict neutralize the power of their wounds, even in cases of enduring horrific violence. These stories speak to our capacity to find peace in our hearts and minds among the chaos of life's volatile journey – dancing with the energy by allowing emotions to flow, being mindful, letting go, recognizing the humanity in those who have caused us harm, speaking our truth, and finding courage to change what is in our power. The stories in this book are sure to touch all readers. Valuable tools for the journey are also offered, which include easily accessible self-care practices to help us find peace in our hearts and minds along the way.

Jennifer Blevins, M.S.W., Director of Brian Coyle Community Center in Minneapolis,
Research Associate, Center for Restorative Justice & Peacemaking, U.M.

Dr. Mark Umbreit offers powerful and moving stories of healing from trauma, whether inflicted by others, by ourselves, or by sickness. This healing is possible when we embark on a journey beyond fear and anger to seek our deepest resources as human beings. The compassion and wisdom that embraces our common humanity, recognizes the suffering of both victim and victimizer, and accepts physical illness and limitation. Umbreit tells of unimaginable trauma and the brave men and women who, using the tools of restorative justice, have stepped beyond the toxins of self-defeating shame and anger. These stories are guideposts, offering direction to each of us as we live our own lives, working with injuries done to us, injuries done by us, and severe health challenges.

Erik Fraser Storlie, PhD, Instructor in Meditation and Mindfulness, Center for Spirituality and Healing, University of Minnesota

This small book beautifully illuminates the power we all have to make profound shifts in the troubles that rob our lives of zest, joy, and fulfillment. Using personal memoirs and stories of anguish, trauma, and woundedness, Umbreit demonstrates again and again how he and others have transformed the toxicity of violation into its life-giving properties.

Marilyn Armour, Ph.D. LICSW, School of Social Work, University of Texas – Austin,
Distinguished Teaching Professor, Director of Institute for Restorative Justice and Restorative Dialogue

In this much needed book Mark shares many stories of courage and strength from within his own life and those he has worked with in numerous states and countries, stories that go far beyond quick fixes and problem solving, stories that are grounded in a transformative journey of the soul, even in the midst of tremendous conflict and even trauma for many. He draws upon the wisdom of the dance, the engagement of energy and healing, from cultures past and present. This is a wonderful guide in exploring the dance and, more importantly, to open up to working with the energy of life to heal our woundedness and stress through daily practices to nurture our body and soul. It offers insight to the unseen spiritual and the seen physical realms. When dancing with the energy, the sixth sense (intuition) and seventh sense (see or feel the future) are strengthened. Keep dancing my Kolas (friends).

Gary Ten Bear, Substance Abuse Counselor, Sun Dancer

INTRODUCTION

The fields of conflict resolution, peacemaking, and trauma healing are loaded with many excellent books, articles, and training manuals. All of these are important resources and provide practical guidance. While these conventional resources, including my own, are necessary, they also are often not sufficient in addressing the power and energy beneath the verbal language of conflict and trauma.

This book offers a very different way of viewing, understanding, and responding to conflicts and traumatic events experienced in our lives. The focus is upon finding strength, compassion, and peace within our lives and hopefully in others. Our peace need not be dependent upon those individuals with whom we are in conflict or the circumstances, unless we choose to give them that power. The book is about becoming aware of and working with the energy of conflict or traumatic events in a way that doesn't focus exclusively on the verbal expression of the conflict. The words of conflict and trauma can become a trap. They can easily cause us to become stuck in the powerful emotions we are trying to avoid.

In all of my previous books, articles, training manuals, and videos on conflict transformation and healing through restorative dialogue, I follow a conventional format of logical and linear sequencing of topics and analysis. Five of these books are grounded in empirical research that I have conducted throughout North

America and other countries. *Dancing with the Energy of Conflict and Trauma* is a very different type of book. With this book, I am attempting to move beyond logical and linear left-brain thinking to the more intuitive, feeling, and circular characteristics of right brain thinking. The format and the process of writing this piece has become for me akin to quilting together the stories of my life, hand-stitching the personal with the professional, the spiritual with the intellectual, and creating a mosaic of my life experiences. This book is anchored in real life struggles with conflict and traumatic events – of others and my own. I will attempt to fully engage the wisdom of the heart as well as the wisdom of the mind. The healing power of story and narrative will be the book's guiding path. The supreme importance of humanizing our adversaries and humbling ourselves will be the book's guiding spirit.

Dancing with the Energy of Conflict and Trauma is neither a training manual nor a definitive textbook. It is offered as a collection of powerful life stories about the search for meaning and wholeness in the midst of conflict and traumatic events, all of which have been part of my life's journey and my work with individuals and groups throughout North America and numerous other countries in Africa, Asia, Europe, and South America.

Dancing with the Energy of Conflict and Trauma is meant to supplement, not replace, existing resources. It offers a window into what many would consider to be one of the most powerful, yet least understood approaches to dealing with severe conflict and trauma - that of embracing and working with the energy that is driving the conflict. The intent is to assist the reader in learning the importance of healthy release of toxic emotional energy that keeps us stuck in patterns of conflict, and learning to let go of our efforts to change other people or difficult circumstances with which we are faced. Learning to focus on the only thing we truly have power to change: ourselves and the energy we bring to what we experience, and learning practices that foster strength and peace within our souls. It means embracing life in its wholeness and nurturing our mind, body, and spirit.

This book will begin with several brief stories of how painful conflict and life threatening traumatic events in my life and others have been and continue to be my greatest teachers; teachers of life wisdom, compassion, and humility. The healing and release found in some stories is totally independent of a dialogue with the person who caused the harm or a cure of the traumatic event or diagnosis. Many other stories involve face-to-face dialogue between the person who was deeply harmed and the perpetrator. All of the stories bear witness to the incredible strength and resilience of the human spirit. *Dancing with the Energy of Conflict and Trauma* is an invitation to expand our awareness of the magic and mystery to be found in walking the path of authentic transformation and healing through directly facing our most difficult conflicts and traumatic experiences.

I will share with you my earliest learnings about the power of working with the emotional energy of conflict and traumatic events, allowing for its full release in myself and others, which I experienced long before I used the language of energy. I will also share my own experience with intense inter-personal conflicts with co-workers and family members, as well as painful intrapersonal conflicts related to life threatening traumatic health related events within our family.

Many real life stories of incredible, yet ordinary people like Karen and Peter, will be offered. People who in the wake of severe conflicts and trauma found inner reservoirs of strength, resilience, and wisdom that led to healing, transformation, and peace after facing their greatest pain. Stories will come from workplace settings, families, within communities, and in war torn nations from Northern Ireland, to Africa, and the Middle East. Nearly all of these stories come from the life journeys of people I have been blessed to befriend and work with from more than twenty-five countries over the past thirty years. In respect to the privacy of the involved parties, the names and specific identifying characteristics of the conflict are altered, unless otherwise noted. These stories stretch the imagination of what can be possible in fostering our own healing. These stories provide powerful testimony to the strength of the human spirit; touching of the soul of humanity in the presence of some of the most evil and violent behavior imaginable.

Later, we will hear from a young Israeli mother who was robbed at knifepoint by Palestinian youth who believes that the trauma of this event was in the end a gift of awakening that lead to a more engaged life. For her and many others we'll hear from, the healing journey is not a quick fix simply based on slogans and five step plans. It requires entering an unfamiliar yet deeply enriching state of being that we are all capable of, despite our backgrounds, our woundedness, our culture, and our education. It requires tapping into the wisdom and life-giving energy that the creator (or whatever other metaphor you choose to use for a higher power) has bestowed upon us to heal. In Western culture we speak of prayer, meditation, love, service, and humility as manifestations of this life-giving wisdom and energy. This energy has been recognized throughout history, both in Western culture and even more so in Indigenous cultures throughout the world. Different words and metaphors are used to describe this creator-given capacity we have to deal with severe conflict and traumatic events.

Whatever words are used, such a healing approach to conflict and traumatic events goes far beyond quick, and often, superficial problem solving, expressions of forgiveness, and written agreements. This approach is grounded in a spirit of compassion and humility. It is ultimately a way a life; a direction rather than a destination.

The book concludes with what we can learn from these courageous individuals, who offer us many gifts of awakening that can enrich our lives and free our spirit. Practical tools for the journey of facing conflict and traumatic events are offered as well. I make no promise that all these tools will work for all people, but many can work for most people if they are used in a way that is sensitive to their life and culture. These "tools for the journey" can empower us in walking the path of finding peace in the midst of the storm, and finding new meaning and wholeness in the many dimensions of our lives.

The people and communities I have worked with from many different cultures and backgrounds in more than twenty-five countries have been among my most important teachers of life wisdom. My role was to serve as a mediator, peacemaker, teacher, trainer, or consultant. My lived experience has been to consistently bear witness to the enormous strength, resilience, and wisdom to be found among even the most wounded from conflict and trauma. The power of their stories has led to this book.

Beginning the Journey:
Anger, Frustration, and Healing

On a beautiful summer day, a county fair was bustling in an average Midwestern town, but in the late afternoon, dark clouds began to hover over the fair, and within minutes rain came pouring down. Peter, a local police officer and a single father of a four-year-old girl, had spent the day drinking beer at the firemen's tent with his buddies. But when the rain came, he rushed for his full-sized, Ford pick-up in the parking lot, along with many other, wet fair-goers. In a drunken fog, Peter became frustrated with the long line of cars and pushed the accelerator down as he swerved to the left in order to shoot past the other automobiles.

Karen and her husband of fourteen years, Rick, were walking on the right side of the road and in the direct path of Peter's two-ton truck. In his intoxicated rush, the off-duty police officer hit the couple, who up until this moment had lived an ordinary middle-class life. Without ever seeing them, Peter injured Karen and killed Rick. He didn't stop; didn't even realize what he had done. Only later, when he heard the call across his police radio, did he understand the gravity of his actions.

Peter confessed, and in due course, the former police officer would be convicted of negligent homicide and sentenced to three years of incarceration.

Conflict and traumatic events are inevitable. The conflict may simply be a nuisance, an inconvenience or a mildly stressful event that is not likely to disturb us for long. Yet many of the conflicts we have encountered or will face in our life's journey are far more severe, often leading to a certain degree of trauma and grief, like seen in the above story of Karen, Rick, and Peter. Such intense conflict and trauma within ourselves, with others, and even within communities and nations can become highly toxic, harmful to our health, and at times lead to violence and bloodshed. We begin to question the meaning of life and our purpose for living.

As we live with the highly toxic residue of conflict, we yearn for freedom from its claws, its emotional and physical consequences. The anger, vulnerability, and fear seem ever present. The constant stress, anxiety, and loss of sleep haunt us. In the words of Bishop Desmond Tutu of South Africa, "Holding onto unresolved intense anger is like taking a daily dose of rat poison and expecting the rat to die." Anger is a valid emotion that can be useful in many ways and can motivate people to take action that has a positive impact on their lives and the lives of others, but it can also be harmful. The inability to, at some point, let go of deep felt anger toward the people with whom conflicts or traumatic events occur, results in dis-ease in our lives, like a cancer metastasizing in our souls, with endless "cell" growth spreading throughout many dimensions of our lives. At best, this can lead to constant moderate stress and unhappiness. At worst, it can lead to severe stress, significant health problems, broken relationships, ever-increasing bitterness and cynicism, and a loss of meaning and direction in one's life, as Karen experienced after the death of her husband, Rick.

Nine months after the incident, I agreed to a request from the local Victim Services Agency to work with Karen. The widow had a desire to talk with the man who had killed her husband, and she contacted me. For more than three decades I have facilitated these kinds of victim/offender dialogues and have trained many hundreds of others in the process. Because Karen had moved after her loss, much of our work together was over the telephone.

As a practitioner and scholar of Qigong, an ancient Chinese healing practice of aligning breath, movement, and awareness, I am quite sensitive to the energy or spirit of others, something that can often even be felt over the telephone. From the start I sensed the energy of anger and impatience from Karen. I listened for a while, then began slowly introducing the process of restorative dialogue in the context of victim-offender trauma, talking about how there would need to be a good deal of separate preparation. I would have to connect with Peter in prison, as well. It could be many months before a meeting could occur, and the meeting might not ever occur. It's very possible that either Peter or Karen would get to a point in the process at which they change their mind about meeting with the other, and for the process to move forward, both parties need to agree to meet.

"This is a voluntary process, not something you force a prisoner to do."

Karen's impatience was urgent and clear, "I want to meet with this guy. NOW. I don't need any preparation. I've lost my husband. My life is in turmoil. I have to meet this PUNK. I don't know why I have to meet him, but I just know I've got to meet with him to free myself."

But there's another side to conflict and trauma. It can become the engine that drives growth and healing within our lives—something that Karen unknowingly hinted at in our first conversation when she said she wanted to "free" herself.

The initial conversation with Karen set in motion many months of groundwork, including several face-to-face preparation meetings with her.

In the midst of all my work with Karen, the widow, I also had to negotiate with three levels of corrections within the criminal justice system, because Peter, as a former police officer, had been transferred from a state prison, where there were inmates he had helped convict, to a federal institution in an adjoining state. I arranged phone conferences with Peter in prison, which, like with Karen, lasted several hours spread out over several months. Ultimately, he agreed to talk with Karen as long as the meeting occurred in the county jail where he previously worked. I met Peter for the first time in person only two days prior to the actual dialogue session in that very county facility.

Before their meeting, Karen never clearly articulated what her expectations were, or why she wanted to talk with this man who had changed her life so tragically and whom she seemed to hate.

4

Earlier in my career, I would have wanted to control the situation more and might have been hesitant to go forward with the case because of this. But over the past thirty-five years I've witnessed the powerful phenomenon of releasing emotional energy and the healing effect it can have. I trusted my gut. I could sense that Karen's healing was very much related to letting go of this toxic energy, talking to Peter and getting answers to her questions.

The widely recognized and embraced serenity prayer offers a helpful daily meditation for the journey, whether you are the person directly dealing with trauma and conflict (Karen or Peter) or a support person to those individuals (me). In reference to a higher power, whatever that higher power might be called in the context of your life and culture:

Grant me the serenity to accept that which I cannot change
(In myself, others, or the circumstances I am faced with),

Grant me the courage to change that which I can
(The choices I make, the attitude and energy I bring to what I am faced with),

And grant me the wisdom to know the difference.
(Comments in parenthesis added by author)

I began the session, as always, with a gentle opening statement inviting Karen to share with Peter her story of the impact

5

of this crime on her life, without any interruptions, and then he would have the same chance to share his perspective. Later, if they wanted, they could discuss any thoughts about repairing the harm, in whatever way, perhaps even symbolic.

Again, the spirit of impatience arose.

Karen interrupted, "Look, I'm not here to tell stories or listen to stories. I've got questions of this punk." She stood up from her chair, breathing heavily, "I just want to talk with this guy."

I looked at Peter, "Are you OK with just jumping into this and getting going?"

Karen was a large woman and even when both were standing she was taller than Peter, an average-sized, working-class, white male.

"Yeah, that's ok. I'm here to help her out in whatever way I can," he replied.

Still looming, with the tone and posture of an aggressive prosecutor, Karen would point at Peter and repeatedly ask, "Why the hell did you do this? Didn't you give any thought to this? You're a cop. Of all people you should know you don't drink the way you were and then drive and then leave the scene of an accident. How the hell could you have done this?"

She asked all kinds of other questions, too.

Peter responded as best he could. He talked about what led up to the tragedy, how he'd never had any issue with drinking and driving before. He said he couldn't believe what he did and that he ran from the scene. He talked about how ashamed he was, how he had thoughts of killing himself, how he held a gun to his head the night it happened.

The words of conflict and trauma are certainly important to address at various points, through deep listening, clarification, greater understanding, and finding common ground. Quick and shallow listening, in the rush of our life, is the ever-present reality in modern life with all of its technology and social networking. Being mindful of our energy and ego, breathing slowly and deep, connecting with the energy of our heart, and saying little prepares us well to listen deeply. Not feeling the need to come up with the perfect response or to remember every word spoken frees us to genuinely connect and be present in the moment with the speaker. Finding serenity in the midst of what may be turbulent emotions through following our breath as it flows deeply within our body is an added benefit of this listening technique.

Learning to work with the emotional energy, our own and others, that fuels conflict is even more important to finding peace within.

Karen and Peter continued talking for over an hour. And then I sensed Karen needed a break. Before leaving the room, she surprised me with a request, "I really want to talk directly with Peter. I'm a cop wannabe. I want to become a law enforcement officer and he's a cop, you know? I just, I want to talk to him; just the two of us."

I looked to Peter and reassured him that he did not have to do this, but he wanted to do it, too. And so when we reconvened, I stayed in a separate, adjoining room, chatting with a friend of Karen's who drove her to the meeting. Through the thin door I could hear the occasional noise. After another hour and a half, the door opened, and Karen walked in.

Her energy was entirely different. She slowly shuffled into the room, with her head down, breathing slowly, offering no comments. Karen slouched in a chair near us.

"He's not a punk. He killed my Rick, but he's not a punk." And after a few more moments of silence she looked up at me again and said, "I can't believe what I just did before coming in here."

And I'm thinking, *oh my God, what did she do?*

And she looked at me and said, "Peter and I had talked about everything…and there's this moment of silence…and I looked up at Peter and I said—I can't believe I did this—I said, 'Do you need a hug?'… And he said, 'Yeah,' with tears in his eyes."

And she went over and hugged this man, who up to then was a punk, the monster who killed her husband.

We went on and debriefed a bit more, most of which was not verbal; it was just being present with Karen, with her totally relaxed energy, just as I had been present with her angry, impatient energy. Her body posture, her tone of voice, and her breathing pattern, were powerful indicators that something energetically had shifted in a big way. Before she had twitched and gasped—now she was relaxed, calm, and spoke with a soft tone of voice.

I then went in and sat down next to Peter, who was still in his chair, almost in a meditative mood, saying nothing, very relaxed, very peaceful. I asked him if he had any regrets about being left alone with Karen.

"No, we needed to talk with each other. You guys have been helpful, but frankly, even before the break we forgot you were there. She needed to let me know the pain I caused in her life, and it was not easy hearing it. I've never felt more powerful feelings of shame within myself in my life." And then he said to me, "Mark, I can't believe what we did at the end."

It's important for the restorative dialogue process to allow time for the turbulence of conflicted feelings, from intense anger and vulnerability to moments of strength and wisdom. It can even result in serenity for some, like Karen and Peter after genuinely "being" with each other and hugging at the end. The time is needed to strongly assert one's needs, to speak one's truth of injustice; time to look within and allow these difficult moments to be our greatest teachers. The process may seem like an endless circle of allowing our emotional energy to flow as it needs to in our quest for healing, taking the lead at times, and at other times just following and accepting the natural course of these difficult conversations with no illusions that we can control the outcome. In other words, we're dancing with the energy of conflict and traumatic events that we will encounter in our life's journey.

Finding peace is not about some blissful state of mind that is far removed from conflicts within our lives or with others. Nor does it have to be dependent upon the actions of others with whom we are in conflict or a dramatic change in circumstances with which we are faced, such as a severe illness, new diagnosis, or chronic disease. Finding peace is about facing the reality of those conflicts and traumatic events; leaning into them with gentleness, befriending them as part of who we are at this moment, reducing their power and toxicity.

Confronting My
Step-Father In-Law:
Doing the Unexpected

I grew up in a loving, middle-class, conservative Christian family in Chicago during the turmoil of the Cold War with Russia, coming of age during the turbulence of the civil rights movement and the war in Vietnam. My journey of understanding and responding to conflict cannot be separated from my life as a young boy growing up in the midst of massive conflict within our nation, widespread injustice, and demands for social change, just as youth of today are facing similar issues.

Within my family, there were periodic conflicts with my older brother and even deeper conflicts with my father; though the story I tell later in this chapter is of a conflict with my step father-in-law. The struggles with my dad and brother did not have lasting toxic power. As a younger man, the most powerful conflicts were within myself as I questioned the meaning of life and my responsibility in the midst of what seemed like so much hypocrisy and injustice, vividly portrayed in so many of the adults I knew and in the media. The beautiful values taught in our schools, churches, families, and greater society were in such contrast to the reality of so much deeply entrenched racism and intolerance in those same bodies.

As a college student in the late 1960s, I joined in the civil rights movement and voter registration drives in the South, precisely because I took seriously the wisdom of my religious upbringing and the message of Jesus: compassion and service to those who are the least among us; reconciliation and healing among those we are in conflict with; forgiveness toward those who have hurt us; advocacy of non-violence, justice and peace; challenging the religious and political status quo; and, little identification with individuals and institutions of power and wealth. It became clear that for most in my conservative Christian community, I took Jesus far too seriously. They saw a prophet of fear and damnation while I saw a wise teacher who challenged the existing powers and cultural norms with tremendous contemporary relevance.

At this young age, I only saw life and spirituality through my own cultural lenses, that of a non-inclusive Christianity. Today I remain connected with my root tradition in a profoundly inclusive manner enriched by my increasing exposure to, and in some cases, practice of the wisdom of other spiritual traditions such as Buddhism and Native American teachings and practices. I have come to believe that the wisdom of Jesus does not in any way cancel out the wisdom of other prophets and teachers who emerged in other cultural settings.

The conflicts and life threatening traumatic events that I will share with you were painful and even frightening, yet without realizing at the time, they taught me powerful lessons about working with the emotional and spiritual energy beneath the verbal language of conflict and the terror of traumatic events. My response to these events certainly wasn't choreographed – it was spontaneous. I didn't run but I didn't fight directly, in the way you might expect. And in the following stories, the emotional

12

turmoil, pain, and even terror was released and transformed into new energy for healing and growth. Learning to work with the energy that drives intense conflicts and trauma is not a systematic, easily teachable process, but I hope these stories will make an initial contribution. Far more will be offered in the last two chapters on recognizing the many gifts of awakening present as we directly face our pain and learn practices to nurture our body and soul.

My earliest teaching about the energy of conflict and the healing journey came out of an argument with my step father-in-law in 1972. Within the first few years of my marriage, my wife and I were visiting her mother in Chicago and her second husband, Pete. My wife, Alexa, and her mom were in a bedroom looking over some new items that had been purchased. I was in the living room with Pete, watching a slide show about Alexa's aunt's missionary work in Africa. As Pete advanced the slides he would periodically make racist comments about the black Africans. After a while he would joke about how he shouldn't use the "N-word" in my presence since I was such a liberal with lofty values. As the slides progressed, his racist comments kept coming as did cheap shots about me being a liberal. I was getting increasingly agitated.

"I don't appreciate you playing games with me about this," I said. "I certainly don't believe these people are N---------s and I find it to be a very offensive term, but I would rather you be honest about your racist feelings than try to be politically correct and saying what you think I want to hear."

"There goes your righteous liberal attitude again," Pete replied.

Things kept escalating, my heart beating faster, my breathing increasingly shallow, and all of a sudden there was a retching from my soul, as if some powerful force within me was seeking a path of release.

I stood up and, totally out of character, yelled, ".....you!" an aggressive swear word at him.

Pete got up; his face was red. He started to move toward me. Then he abruptly turned around and left the room.

I stood there in disbelief, waiting for him to attack me. I sat back in the chair, stunned at what I had said, terrified of the implications for our family relations, particularly since my wife and mother-in-law in the next room must certainly have heard this outburst.

Pete came back in the room, said nothing, and continued the remainder of the slide show. The rest of the evening was tense, with few words exchanged.

As the evening was wrapping-up, Pete and Alexa's mom walked us down to the parking area in the basement of their building. With a sense of awkwardness and tension we began to say goodbyes. I could not even look at Pete. He moved toward me, said goodbye in a reasonably friendly manner, and gave me a bear hug.

Yes, I said a bear hug. Never before had I ever received a hug from Pete. Never before had I ever swore at him or any other member of our family. From that point on the tone and reality of our relationship changed in a good way. From then on, I felt a sense of respect even though we had very different perspectives on life, religion, race, politics, and culture.

Looking back, my explosive encounter with my step father-in-law represented a powerful shift in the energy of our relationship. My outburst triggered something in Pete that allowed him to let go of some of the toxic energy he carried related to his stereotype about me as a weak, liberal do-gooder. From that point on, we were okay with each other, sharing a beer now and then.

I cannot come up with a clear rational explanation for what occurred. This was far more than a healthy release of anger, a so-called cathartic effect. The very nature of our relationship changed. Yet from the perspective of trying to understand the emotional energy behind our actions it makes sense. The words were the triggering event yet it was the spontaneous explosion of toxic energy that was the tipping point to establishing an entire different relationship between the two of us. This would never have happened if Pete and I had civilly "talked out" our different perspectives and values.

I want to be very clear in saying that what I just described is not a prescription for how to address family conflict. Yelling an aggressive swear word at your step father-in-law is not conducive to healthy conflict management. Yet, it is precisely because what I did was so totally opposite of my normal behavior that it shifted the blending of our energies in a huge way and, as unlikely as it would seem, led to more respect between us and a sense of healing within our relationship. The lesson here is recognizing the disarming power of doing the unexpected, not yelling at another person. Had my explosive angry words been part of my normal behavior, this conflict would likely have escalated leading to far more damage in the relationship. Normally, I coach people in conflict to take a slow, deep breath, center themselves, and respond from a calm place. But sometimes yelling might be just the thing. Doing the unexpected can be a powerful practice in shifting the energy of conflict and disarming the other party.

The Near Death of Our Young Daughter:
Embracing Life

It was 1984. Laura, our precious six-year-old daughter, was diagnosed with encephalitis, a swelling of the brain that put her into a coma. Our lives stopped. In the coming weeks and months our lives were filled with intense pain, fear, hopelessness, vulnerability, grief, and glimmers of hope.

My wife Alexa and I lived out of a Ronald McDonald House for several weeks in Chicago. We were told Laura had a 6% chance of living and if she survived she would be extremely disabled. Facing the likely death of our precious six-year-old daughter triggered a range of powerful thoughts and conflicted feelings. Why us? How could this happen if God is a loving God? How do we deal with our older daughter Jenni when all of our attention is now focused on Laura? What kind of life will we have if Laura dies? Will we ever be able to return to a so-called normal life? Is life even worth living when our precious, beautiful, and innocent little girl is taken from us?

Up until this point, I never realized how emotional pain could manifest itself. When I returned to the Ronald McDonald House in the evening after our time with Laura in the hospital

17

intensive care unit, I tried to sleep. I vividly remember feeling sharp pain in my abdomen, as if a dagger was in my gut.

For three weeks, we spent each and every day in Laura's room in the intensive care unit. Laura was totally un-responsive, yet we believed she could hear voices. Alexa and I would continually talk to her, tell her about activities at school and in the neighborhood and read her messages from friends and family. We would periodically massage her muscles. One evening I was next to her bed, leaning over the guardrail, holding her little palm to my cheek, and telling her to use every ounce of her stubbornness to fight this illness and come back to her family. As I was feeling her gentle little palm on my cheek, I felt her hand move. I assumed it was a muscle spasm. But I felt it again and all of a sudden I felt her grasp my neck, pull me down to her face, and wrap her little arm around my neck. The joy I felt within my heart is indescribable. My precious little baby was coming back to life! I was in awe of the miracle that was happening. As tears poured from my eyes, I saw Alexa and our friend hug each other, jumping for joy, and celebrating in the miracle we were witnessing. Laura would not let go of me for several minutes. My back was twisted leaning over the guardrail of the bed, but I didn't care. Finally she let go and her eyes opened. She could not speak clearly but was certainly beginning to come out of the coma.

Laura was moved from the intensive care unit to a private room with constant monitoring and care. She began to talk and respond to our voices and touch. Each day that passed, Laura gained more strength and expressive ability, even though she had to relearn how to walk and now had some vision issues that required glasses. But no massive brain damage appeared to have occurred, despite the earlier warnings of doctors about potential consequences. Her doctors and nurses would periodically come in to check on her and many openly referred to the miracle that occurred.

No greater pain can ensue in parents than the likely or actual death of their young child. This traumatic event was a powerful lesson on facing a hard reality, and our own heavy conflicted feelings, yet finding peace in the power of prayer and those who sent loving energy for our family from all over the world. It was a lesson early in our lives about the supreme importance of being mindful of our own energy and taking care of ourselves so that we could be of service to Laura, our older daughter Jenni, and care for each other. Without consciously realizing it at the time, the wisdom of the serenity prayer provided strength for this episode in our life's journey. We desperately yearned for serenity in accepting the fact that we could not change or control the reality of Laura's life threatening illness. We found the courage to change the only thing we could, our choices and attitude about her illness. We would not allow ourselves to become overrun with anger, sadness, and depression- it was imperative for us to find the courage to seize life, to embrace each moment, to channel every ounce of our energy to the healing of Laura.

Parenting a Rebellious Child:
Letting Go of Your Ego

F ew parents are prepared for the powerful and at times dangerous energy of adolescence. Our daughter Jenni did exactly what many adolescents do: She tested limits, and tried to differentiate herself from her parents in search of her own identity. Perhaps because she came from a very loving, open, stable, dialogue-oriented family, Jenni explored the darker side of life. The years of her adolescence were frightening to her mother and me. We felt as if her beautiful gentle spirit had died and she was now possessed by some evil type of energy. I am not talking about messy rooms, violating curfew or skipping school. Jenni was connecting with a new group of "friends" and engaging in activities that were illegal and could be life-threatening. Drugs were certainly part of this.

On an evening in the winter of her thirteenth year of life as we attempted to have a meal together, one of my most profound lessons of dealing with the energy of painful conflict was to emerge. Alexa, our younger daughter Laura, Jenni and I sat at the table eating in 1989. Few words were exchanged. It felt strained and awkward. Jenni, dressed in all black – her clothes were decorated with every swear word that might push a parent's button - sat next to me, but she was pulled back as far as she could.

After many minutes of silence, Jenni leaned toward me in an aggressive posture, glared into my eyes, and screamed "I hate you. I hate you, I hate you!!!"

Hearing these words deeply hurt me. I felt disrespected, and attacked. My ego kicked in and I thought of grounding her for months and telling her to stop this behavior. Somehow I was able to take a deep breath; see her as the precious baby who entered this world and brought us so much joy; connect with my deep feelings of love for her; and, focus on my hope to make it through this turbulent time of her life without fracturing our relationship in ways that would take years to overcome, if ever. I was able to keep my mouth shut. I allowed the toxic energy of her words of hatred to flow uninterrupted. I did not absorb them in my heart, but instead drew them out of her through my attentive silence and presence and then let them bounce off and away from me.

After many moments of her shouting, "I hate you! I hate you!" and not receiving a counter aggressive verbal message from me, she stopped. Her body relaxed as if it had let go of some weighty energy.

It was silent for a few seconds. I leaned toward her and said, in a calm and caring voice, "Jenni, when you say you hate me, do you mean me your dad or is it about all the stuff you are dealing with at school and with friends? What's really going on?" I paused and allowed for silence, for space for her to find her voice.

Jenni began to talk in a softer voice, saying that her life was so screwed up. I listened and I told her we would like to hear more about what is going on in her life. I asked if she would feel better going into the other room and sitting around the fireplace. Laura went to play in her room, while Alexa and I just listened to whatever Jenni felt safe enough to share with us. As a parent it was not easy hearing about the drugs and violence at her school and the sexual activity of twelve and thirteen-year-old kids, her "friends."

Many times I had the urge to interrupt her, to ask her why she didn't think about this or that. I had to work hard to tame my ego, to just listen with love and compassion for this precious young woman rather than react or give advice. Periodically I took deep breaths that helped me to remain emotionally present with her in a nonjudgmental spirit, to disengage from the anger and judgment of my ego, which would have closed down any possibility of her feeling safe enough to let us know what was really going on in her life. Jenni told us quite a bit, and gave us a real glimpse into her struggles that up to then had been her heavily guarded secrets.

Many tears were shed. The aggressive angry voice of Jenni telling me she hated me transformed into the more gentle voice of a vulnerable and troubled young woman trying to find meaning in her life and relationships. Highly toxic and hurtful energy had been transformed into authentic communication between a rebellious young daughter and her parents. The energy of the entire event had shifted in a very palpable way. Were all of her issues "dealt with" and fixed? Absolutely not. There was no attempt at problem solving that evening. Was the toxic energy of this event cleared for the moment so that our family could touch our deeply felt love for one another and avoid the typical escalation of similar parent-child encounters? Without question, yes!

How did we overcome our urge to react in anger to our daughter? Was it because of my intellectual wisdom communicated through my verbal messages? I doubt it. Was it because Alexa and I had pre-planned such an event and worked on a strategy that we believed would be effective? No. Parental anger in this situation would be totally understandable. Yet, our response was anchored in our love for Jenni and our intuitive sense that she needed a safe place to express her anger, her pain, her struggle for meaning in her life.

The toxic energy of Jenni erupted. Rather than blocking the release of that energy through my verbal and non-verbal response as a defensive and righteously offended parent, I was able to put my own ego aside so that Jenni's anger could be released. My silence gave her the necessary space. There seemed to be a blending of our energies that was disarming, that caused no additional harm to our relationship or to either of us. Instead, the energy of this intense and hurtful communication between a parent and a child was shifted from intense anger to a renewed opportunity for intimacy and connection.

Allowing the release of Jenni's anger toward me, no matter how painful it was to hear, was clearly the turning point in rebuilding our relationship. After all these years, Alexa and I treasure the healthy adult relationship we have with Jenni, her husband, and two young children. She is an incredible person, wife, teacher, parent, daughter, and friend. There is no residue of bad parent-child stuff from her rebellious adolescent days that haunt us. It was our ability to listen deeply, to hear the pain beneath the words of hatred, to allow for silence, to refrain from saying a lot, to stay connected to our love for her, and to stay focused on our primary concern to help her through this turbulent and dangerous stage of her life that led to our deep friendship today.

Conflicts at My Job:
Deep Listening and Breathing to Serenity

I was totally consumed with preparing a grant proposal to fund our program to service victims of crime, ex-offenders, and prisoners. Being an Administrator of a non-profit community service agency, I had often found myself in this position. As I rushed to check with another colleague about specific objectives to include in the proposal, I was met in the hall by Carol, a young woman whom I supervised. She approached me for help.

"Mark, I have a very difficult victim-offender mediation case that the judge referred. I need to get your advice," she asked.

Even in my busyness, I tried to focus my attention and listen to Carol. My mind, however, was still on the grant proposal. After several minutes I offered her a few helpful thoughts and continued on to the office of the colleague I was planning to meet with. Even though Carol interrupted my chain of thought, I felt good about being able to help her. Later that day, Carol saw me again in the office mail area. No one else was present.

She said: "Mark, when I talked with you earlier today I was really disappointed. I needed your help. I respect you. But, you just weren't present with me. Your mind was somewhere else."

Wow! I thought I was helpful and said the right things, I first thought.

Thankfully, I was able to curb any immediate defensiveness and say to Carol, "I'm really sorry. I would really like to hear more about this. Could we go into the back conference room and talk about it, without any interruptions from other people or phones?"

As I sat and listened to Carol's concerns and how she felt about my so-called "helpfulness" in our morning brief conversation, I felt the powerful energy of defensiveness revving up. I had the frequent urge to explain myself, to point out that I was preoccupied with completing a grant proposal to fund her program, or I had several other staff requesting my presence in an unscheduled meeting that would keep me from completing the work I needed to get done or "blah, blah, blah."

It was all true. I had these other real obligations of course, but talking about them would merely communicate the powerful energy of defensiveness.

Fortunately, I was able to take a few deep breaths and be mindful of the fact that Carol had a tremendous need to simply vent, to release stressful energy and concerns that she was carrying. And, I could see, she was probably right. My mind was on the grant even as I tried to respond to her. She didn't need someone defending their actions and attempting to problem solve for her. I kept my mouth closed and just listened—deeply listened—for about forty minutes. As it appeared that her concerns had been expressed and the energy of her language released, I again apologized and said a few words about how I appreciated learning more about her perspective, and about the unintended negative consequences of my behavior. We agreed to meet later in the week and develop some plans for how to avoid this in the future.

Carol had the courage to directly confront me as her supervisor in a respectful manner. I found the strength to curb my defensiveness and deeply listen to Carol's concerns. Once again the toxic energy of this conflict was released and prevented from building up and disrupting our organization's ability to function. Deep listening, not quick problem solving, defused the toxic energy of the conflict. Carol and I continued to work well together, respected each other, and carried on a healthy professional relationship for many years.

Several years later, at a different job in 1984, I was confronted with the most intense and difficult workplace conflict I had ever experienced. I had worked for three years as a consultant and trainer for Steve, the President of a criminal justice reform agency. From the beginning, he and I enjoyed working together. We shared very similar values and approaches to serving crime victims, offenders, and promoting restorative justice in the community. The mutual respect and fun we had working together led Steve to actively recruit me to become his Vice-President, a new position he was developing.

Eventually the person in this new position would likely become President, following Steve's planned retirement. I was told I could help shape the position and that he was open to meeting my needs so that it would work for my entire family, who would be moving to a different state. Negotiation over the final job description, salary, and benefits went extremely well and I was excitedly anticipating this shift in my role with the agency, from periodic consultant to full time Vice-President.

The first year went well. All of the energy, fun, and respect from our previous work together continued. Or so I thought. Long before I spoke of "dealing with the energy of conflict" I experienced it out of my own desperation, stress, and disappointment. I quickly learned that the emotional energy in a relationship between a respected and independent consultant is quite different than that experienced within a manipulative and dysfunctional supervisory relationship.

The energy of control, micro-management, and disrespect became an increasingly present reality at my new job. As the intensity of this conflict grew, I felt as though an emotional cancer was spreading throughout my entire being. It affected other aspects of my life, and consumed nearly all of my thoughts and energy. It humbled me to see that my attempts at rational dialogue and problem-solving with a respected colleague had little impact.

The wisdom of the serenity prayer became a daily meditation. As I reflected on finding serenity in accepting that which I cannot change - the behavior of Steve - and focusing on finding the courage to change that which I could - myself - the full emotional power of the conflict began to lessen.

Out of a sort of instinct and desperation, I found myself continually trying to breathe deeper and more slowly. Somehow in my moments of prayer and meditation I was able to reflect on the prior relationship with Steve and, more importantly, feel the emotional energy of the prior relationship, the respect, fun, and creativity. Feeling even small bits of the emotional energy of our prior relationship humanized the conflict in a manner that took most, but not all, of the toxic energy out of it.

Taking the time to breathe and allowing myself the space to feel also somehow humbled me. I could begin to see my own contribution to the conflict. If not through the words I spoke to Steve, perhaps through the energy behind those words, the tone of voice, the posture of my body. I could begin to see that my actions were likely experienced by Steve as disrespectful and un-warranted.

I tried again and again to rationally talk through conflict and solve the problem by clarifying my role and the expectations that we each had for one another. My mind relied on problem solv-ing skills. I wanted to talk it out. Let's try to find some common ground, a plan to move on.

When I engaged in those verbal problem-solving sessions with my supervisor, it appeared as though we were making some positive movement each time we talked. Yet I felt an increasing tightness in my chest. I felt my breathing becoming very shallow. As we talked, I found my mouth becoming exceedingly dry. Un-comfortably dry.

At first I ignored these messages from my body and wondered if I was getting sick. As the problem solving efforts went on and these bodily reactions kept intensifying, finally it dawned upon me, my body was trying to tell me something. Stop. You must get some space before you proceed. My body was clearly giving me a pow-erful message that easily trumped what my mind was telling me.

If I had depended on or required Steve's willingness to apologize, and to negotiate in good faith a reasonable way of continuing to work together, I would probably still be waiting. I would be carrying toxic, life consuming energy of this conflict with me for many years. It would have continued to negatively affect other aspects of my life and led to a far more cynical at-titude about life and work. No formal conflict resolution ever happened between us. To this day I have no idea if Steve was ever able to own his "stuff," that is, his controlling and disrespectful attitude to me and a number of other staff. What I do know is that focusing on the only thing I could control in this conflict - my own energy, attitude, breath, and choices - not only lessened the effect of the conflict within my life, it also contributed to tremendous emotional growth, new opportunities, self-awareness, humility, and a richer sense of meaning, wholeness, and peace in my continuing life journey.

More than twenty-five years later I look back on this intense, painful conflict with gratitude towards Steve. The timing of this conflict fit within a tiny window of opportunity that allowed my life and work to be catapulted into an entirely different and far more meaningful arena of life work, that of founding the Center for Restorative Justice & Peacemaking at the University of Minnesota and actively engaging in peace building among many diverse communities and cultures in the United States, as well as with twenty-five other countries. This intense conflict was a gift of awakening to enter a far more meaningful and exciting path of my life's journey.

Road Rage:
Confronting Aggression

E arly in the life of our family a frightening act of road rage occurred that could have easily led to a physical assault. My wife Alexa and I, and our daughters, who were six and three at the time, were driving to a cottage that had been owned by my family for several generations. The best summers of my boyhood were spent with my grandmother at this cottage. Mine and Alexa's relationship, which is now going on forty plus years, began as childhood sweethearts at the cottage and in the little village in which it's located. Going back there as young parents with our young children was like returning to a time in the past, loaded with images of safety, love , peace, nature, and lots of friendly neighbors.

We were anxious to get there. The girls were in the car. As I pulled off the highway onto the small road that led into the quiet resort area of our cottage by Lake Michigan, I noticed a large pick-up truck ahead. I was traveling at about fifteen miles per hour, the speed limit, but the truck was only going about five miles per hour. I approached him quickly.

Excited to arrive at the cottage, I swerved to the left to pass him, but then he swerved to the left to block me. I patiently waited a few minutes and then tried again. And again he swerved to the left to block me. I knew a stop sign was coming up shortly as we entered the resort area, so I just patiently drove very slowly behind him. We stopped. I waited for him to proceed. The large pick-up did not move.

After several more minutes, I noticed the driver's side door open. Out came an angry, mean-looking guy moving quickly toward my car. When he arrived at my open window, he started yelling, "You S.O.B.! You were tailgating me! Get the hell out of your car!"

I became numb. I couldn't believe what was happening, and in front of my wife and two young daughters. My mind went through a number of rational thoughts, wanting to believe that I could come up with a rational solution.

Perhaps I should hit the gas pedal and get out of there? No, he could easily catch me. We should definitely lock our doors in the most inconspicuous manner possible.

And, we did so.

Slowly, it dawned on me that the thoughts in my mind would have little impact on dealing with his angry, aggressive energy. Somehow I sensed that taking a deep breath would help me deal with this.

My intuition led me to maintain direct eye contact with him and in a soft non-aggressive voice tone said "I think you're right. I probably was tailgating you. Sorry, I tend to do that at times."

He kept yelling at me, cursing, and trying to get me out of the car. He clearly wanted a fight. Asserting my "rights" and the wrongness of his perception, while on the one hand totally justifiable, would have simply escalated the tension of the moment. I again told him that I was sorry for tailgating him. This went back and forth several times and finally he just stomped on the ground, swore, and then returned to his truck and sped off. I was in shock. Though relieved that the incident was over, the threat of a nasty physical assault, in the last place in the world I would have ever expected it, also left me feeling vulnerable.

Looking back on this event, I cannot give you a clear rational explanation of what happened. It certainly had little to do with the wisdom of my words or the effectiveness of the mediation and negotiation techniques I had learned. It had everything to do with the blending of our energies, doing the unexpected, returning his aggressive energy with an entirely different energy of acquiescence and respect that disarmed him. His angry aggressive energy was immobilized by my non-aggressive energy, without harming or disrespecting him. This event occurred long before I understood the power of working with the energy of conflict. To this day it remains one of the most profound teachings I have ever received, from the most unlikely character I can imagine.

Power Struggle with Agency Founder:
Sweating Through It

Rick is a former professional football player, having even played in the Super Bowl. In his community he is a legend, not only for his athletic talent, but also for his passionate commitment to working with youth. He is not merely a leader in his local African American community—his influence has been felt throughout many communities in his state, and in the many other states where he has spoken and offered training seminars.

Rick, and a friend who played with him in the NFL, established a youth service non-profit agency. Rick was committed to doing the hands-on work with the kids in the community, as a community organizer and youth advocate. He paid little attention to the administrative needs of the organization he founded, trusting the details to others.

When founded, the organization consisted of an entirely African American board of directors. Rick initially served as the Executive Director (ED), but after a few years he gave over leadership to a new person with more administrative experience and talent. Rick was glad to yield all administrative tasks to her.

Rick fairly quickly noticed the new ED had a different management style. One day as he picked-up his office mail, he noticed a pink slip. It said he was being docked for 1.75 hours of pay. At first, he thought this must be some kind of joke. Rick's work required him to be out in the community as much as possible, particularly with young people. In fact, he didn't even think in terms of "nine to five." He felt he needed to be available to the kids and their families whenever he was needed – day or night, weekday or weekend.

The issue of the pink slip in his company mailbox caused Rick quite a bit of concern, especially once he realized it probably wasn't a joke.

The six foot tall 250 pound, proverbial gentle giant went into his new ED's office and asked, "What is this about? Docking me 1.75 hours?"

The new director, in absolute seriousness looked at him and said, "Rick, you need to set a better example for the young people on our staff. You were not in by nine the other day. You came in a bit late."

Trying to control the anger building inside him, Rick took a few deep breaths and said, "What do you mean? I put in way more hours than the forty I'm compensated for."

And she responded, "Well, that might be, but I don't see it. I need to *see* you here in this office. And the fact is that you periodically are not here from nine to five and you don't sign out as you're required."

Rick was losing his composure, "Do you have any idea what my work as a community youth advocate entails? The least effective I can be is to be chained to a desk. The core of my work is about being out in the community."

But the director was unrelenting, "Well, I don't see that. You need to be here NINE to FIVE. And if you do go out, you need to sign out and sign back in. That's what accountability is, and we need to set a good example for the young staff in our agency."

Given the kind of feedback he was receiving, Rick felt he was on the verge of an emotional explosion. *Here he was the FOUNDER of the agency and his very commitment was being questioned by this new member of HIS team!* He thought about how he spent hour upon hour raising money for the agency from donors by negotiating with them at events like the annual week-end NFL golf tournament. Faced with all these negative thoughts and emotions, Rick decided to leave the ED's office before he said something that would make things even more uncomfortable. But as the day progressed, Rick increasingly became more consumed with the disrespect he felt as a result of this conflict.

The next day when he arrived at the office, his muscles and chest were tight and his breath was becoming shallow. It was almost as if his body was saying to him "Don't go in."

That day and for the rest of the week Rick tried to do his best to respond positively to the director's request, but he had a very difficult time doing so. Something just did not feel right.

Eventually, another board member suggested that Rick and the ED go into a mediation session to work this out. The session began with the mediator introducing himself and allowing each person to tell his/her story. In the end, the new director and Rick developed a written agreement. The session did take some of the edge off the conflict; but, unfortunately, it ultimately had little effect in actually resolving it. The root of the conflict lingered.

37

For months Rick became ill in ways he normally did not. As an athlete Rick was accustomed to being aware of his physical body, and he felt his body was clearly responding to the conflict. When he would talk with friends, many advised him to be proactive, even aggressive.

"Rick, play all of your cards. You have the credibility with the funding sources. You are the founder of the agency, the personality and face of this organization."

Some believed the director's behavior was racially motivated and advised Rick to "go after that white lady," even to "blow her out of the water." They reminded him of his connections with the media. Hinting at the racial overtones perceived in the situation, one friend commented that "this could make a very interesting story on the six o'clock news."

Yet, the more he thought about it, Rick wondered about the advice he was receiving. If he attacked this woman and "won" in the media, would he feel vindicated? Would he feel better in his heart, in his body? Would it relieve the stress and dis-ease he was feeling?

While still mulling over what to do, a Native American friend of Rick's invited him to come into the local Native community and participate in a healing sweat lodge. His friend spoke of the benefits of cleansing the conflict from his mind, his soul, and his body through sweat and prayers. Rick had never been to a Native American ceremony before, so naturally he was a little reticent, but desiring a healthy end to this situation, he decided to do it.

On the evening of the sweat, twelve people crawled on hands and knees into the lodge, an act of humility required by Native American tradition. As the entrance to the lodge was closed, the darkness became absolute, the heated rocks glowed red, and the temperature began to rise. Rick felt a powerful sense of healing in the presence of his Native American brothers as they offered prayers on his behalf, speaking in Ojibwa and Lakota. After the three-hour ceremony, the former NFL player and his sweat lodge brethren shared in the time-honored human tradition of sharing a potluck meal.

The evening of the sweat lodge marked a turning point for Rick. He realized that what he needed at the deepest level was not to aggressively fight it out with the new director. What he needed was healing within his soul, and healing within his body. He began going to sweat lodges periodically.

Rick firmly believes the experience to be central to his healing from the conflict. He told his friends that he had chosen not to fight it out, not to garner the support of the media and funding sources, even though it was fairly clear he would be the winner. He rejected that path because he realized the cost of such a victory would not lead to peace within his heart.

Instead Rick chose the path of healing. While verbally talking the situation through in a mediator's presence helped, it did very little to shift the energy of the ongoing conflict. Today, as Rick reflects back many years later, he has no regrets for the path he chose. In fact, he sees that the conflict taught him so much.

Rick does not use the word "energy" explicitly; yet the metaphors he does use clearly indicate a shifting in the relationship between this woman, the agency, and himself. Rather than getting stuck in the toxic energy of anger and hostility, he chose the path of healing within himself and his body. In doing so, he freed himself from the burden he had been carrying. After shifting the energy and embracing a path of healing, Rick also carries on a renewed and respectful relationship with the director.

Rick's story, while unique to his own life and circumstances, has enormous implications for every one of us, in our individual lives, our families, among friends, and in the workplace. We all are confronted with conflicts that often times can become toxic and all consuming. These conflicts can affect our physical health, as well as our emotional health. It's so easy to become defensive, to allow our egos to dictate our actions, to act out on what we believe are our rights, and to push firmly and aggressively against the person we view as the attacker. Rick's story can teach us much about finding peace at the deepest level, allowing the toxic energy of conflict and traumatic events to be released.

Domestic Violence:

Reclaiming Your Power and Releasing Your Abuser

Megan was a participant in a weeklong workshop on forgiveness and healing I was conducting. The workshop is highly experiential. It's not a series of lectures. People aren't sitting in rows, writing notes. We use the circle process, creating a safe, if not sacred, space where students can engage in the deepest form of learning, connecting with the wisdom of the heart, as well as the wisdom of the mind. This is a rare phenomenon in academia. As the workshop proceeded, and as Megan practiced centering through meditation, breath work, yoga stretches, and Qi Gong movements, she increasingly opened up. She talked about her own journey and struggle with issues of forgiveness and healing.

Megan spoke to others in the circle about her marriage, about the young man who she loved and had traveled around the world with, exploring life in other cultures together. She went on to speak of how dramatically things had changed. She detailed how the husband she loved had turned into a monster, who had continually hurt her through physical violence and emotional abuse. She feared for her life and that of her child, and finally had to move out.

The court had issued restraining orders against her husband to maintain separation, but these hadn't helped her feel safe nor at peace. Megan still felt the energy of his violence whether he was present or not. She openly talked about the enormous struggle she felt trying to forgive him, to find her own strength, after he shattered her sense of safety. She wanted to live without the fear of whether she or her daughter would wake up alive the next morning.

During the final workshop closing circle, after an extended period of centering and being present with each other, participants were invited to share what the workshop experience had been for them, to explain what they would be taking with them. As they passed the "talking piece" each person took their turn to speak.

When the talking piece came to Megan she held it in the palms of her hand and stroked it. Even with her head bowed, I could see tears welling up in her eyes. But then a beautiful broad smile blazed across her face and she told us how, having learned the techniques of centering, working with breath, working with the energy of her body through yoga and Qi Gong, she felt transformed.

She said for the first time in years she felt fully connected to her spiritual core. She felt no longer victimized by the ever-present claws of her absent husband's energy of violence and trauma. She also recognized the woundedness in her husband, in the man she loved, in a man who was suffering far more than she ever realized. Being able to view her husband as a human as opposed to a monster allowed Megan to see more of her own strength and freed her from her own fear and suffering. She said that now, whenever she starts feeling the trauma again she would focus on her breath, breathing in slowly, deeply within her belly, holding the breath for a second or two, and then slowly exhaling.

She felt this practice immediately shift the energy in her. The trauma would not lead her into further depressive thoughts. Rather, her new way-of-being shifted her state of consciousness in a way that she felt as if she was reclaiming her power, and her capacity to be fully present -- both for herself and for her daughter.

Megan is one of millions of women who suffer the painful reality of domestic violence in its various and multiple forms. There are few types of conflict that have deeper claws in the victim than domestic violence. The violence itself is often times easier to tolerate than the continual control of the mind and personal behavior the victim feels. Megan used the police and courts to hold her husband accountable, as much as this is realistically possible. Yet this did not make her feel safe.

Megan's choices indicated a passionate embrace of the wisdom found in the Serenity Prayer - letting go and finding peace. Megan found serenity in accepting that which she could not change. She could not change her husband's behavior. In finding the courage to change that which she could, she found the strength to focus on her own energy, her own choices, and the attitude and energy she brought to all that she faced. And she found the wisdom to know the difference between trying to change someone else and finding the power in oneself to deal with one's own energy and choices.

Meeting Their Burglar:
Releasing and Transforming Toxic Energy

The Smith's home had been burglarized by a twenty-year-old man named Steve while they were gone for the weekend. The neighbors had called them when the police arrived. Mr. and Mrs. Smith had to travel back to their home in the city from their cabin in the country. They were furious.

Steve, the offender, was arrested. He admitted his guilt, and the judge, before sentencing him, referred him to a restorative justice program called Victim Offender Mediation that I had developed and then supervised in a large mid-western city. Carol, one of our staff members, initiated the process. She met with the offender first, before even contacting the victims, to check out if he had truly owned up to his crime and was willing to enter a mediation process, to talk about what happened and to develop a plan to repair the harm. He was, although he had many reservations about it. He felt the Smiths were claiming far more damage than he actually did.

Carol called the Smiths, listened to their concerns, and tried to set up a meeting with them. Mr. Smith was extremely angry. He would refer to those "stupid punks" that broke into his home. He talked about how he had been ripped off two times before and it's probably the same idiot that did it again. His anger prevented him from hearing what Carol was saying about the program.

But eventually he listened and said, "Well, let me give it a little more thought and call me back next week."

Carol called him back the following week and he finally agreed, "Why don't you come out to our home, and we'll be glad to tell you more about how it affected us, and we want to learn more about the program."

So Carol, the mediator, went out to their home, did a lot of deep listening, slowly explaining the program in a gentle and down-to-earth way.

Eventually Mr. Smith said, "Yeah, I do, I want to tell that punk what it's like to be victimized, what it's like to have all your stuff taken."

Sue added, "Well, I know my husband wants to do this, but I don't. So he'll do it by himself."

When Carol got back to the office the next day, she checked in with me and asked for my assistance. The high level of anger by both parties was frightening to her. I agreed to co-facilitate the meeting.

Mr. Smith indicated that he preferred having the mediation at a local library conference room in his neighborhood. When we came together at the library with Steve, it was a very tense moment, very awkward. We met each other in the hallway initially.

Mrs. Smith was with her husband. And we weren't expecting that. She made it clear that she was concerned her husband would "lose It" and she needed to be there in case he needed to be dragged out of the room.

Despite some hesitancy, we proceeded. There were no handshakes, just brief verbal introductions. We went into the conference room. It was huge, with no tables. We had hoped that there would be tables for people to sit around so there would be some clear boundaries, but we had to sit in just an open circle.

When all were seated, Carol began with some brief comments about what we'll be doing this evening, inviting their participation, thanking them for coming. I then added a few comments about the opportunity to take a break at any time and then I opened up the process by turning to Mr. Smith and inviting him to speak directly to Steve about how he felt about what happened. He needed little prompting. He was rocking in the chair, arms folded on his chest. Steve was slouched in his chair with his eyeballs glaring at the carpet, looking like he had no interest whatsoever in being there.

The energy of Mr. Smith's presence was full of anger.

Within four minutes the anger got so high, with him calling Steve a punk and other names, that I was just about ready to intervene and redirect the conversation, to essentially break the energy of his explosiveness and ask Steve to share his story.

But before I did that, Steve actually was getting so agitated by this that he jumped out of his seat and he said, "This is a bunch of shit. I shouldn't have come."

I in turn jumped out of my chair and looked at Steve and said, "Steve, I can understand you wanting to go. Mr. Smith is very angry, but I know that he and his wife are here because they want to learn more about what happened. They want to learn more about you and they want to see if some plan to repair the harm can be worked out that seems fair. Can you give it a few more minutes, and then if it's just not working, go ahead and leave?"

That appeared to be enough to validate his anger and to encourage him to stick around a little.

This was truly the beginning of my learning of the healing power of releasing toxic emotional energy in conflicts. The outburst of anger by both Steve and Mr. Smith was probably the most pivotal moment in the entire mediation session. It was a transformative event. Beforehand, their body language was closed. Their voice tone was high and intense. But after the verbal explosion of their emotional energy, they both sat up a little more erect, their tone of voice was significantly lower. Mr. Smith began asking Steve questions in a very direct way. Steve actually looked openly at him.

Incredible as this might sound, after about forty-five minutes there were some moments of silence in the midst of this intense verbal exchange. Mr. Smith leaned toward his wife, who was sitting a little behind him and they whispered. Carol and I were wondering what in the world was going on. But we didn't interrupt. We sensed, at an intuitive level, something very powerful was going on.

After they whispered to each other, Mr. Smith looked at Steve, bent over closer to him, and in a soft voice tone, said, "Do you know our daughter Sara?"

"Yeah," the young man replied.

"Was she involved in this? I mean, did she set you guys up to hit our place?"

"No, Sara's a good kid. She was not involved at all."

And then Mr. Smith leaned back toward his wife and they whispered again.

He turned and looked straight at Steve, leaned forward even more closely and in a softer voice tone said, "Do you ever see

Sara? Ever since she ran from that drug treatment program we haven't seen her for the past year."

Steve indicated that he sees her every now and then.

Mr. Smith, the angry, furious victim looked at Steve, the criminal, the convicted felon and pleaded, "Next time you see Sara, could you tell her that her mom and dad really love her. We miss her. And tell her we'd love her to come home."

I was bearing witness to the most incredible energetic shift in major conflict that I had ever witnessed. The energy of tension, awkwardness, anger and hostility, which was so present at the beginning, had now shifted to a very different, gentler form of communication in which the victims were seeking help in their parenting from the criminal. It was a process of mutual aid. Steve was no longer the convicted felon, the burglar. He was a guy that messed up and who was at some level connected with their daughter who they were estranged from. And they needed Steve to help them reconnect with their daughter Sara.

Following discussion of the full impact of the burglary on all involved, the issue of actual losses and the need for restitution were addressed. A restitution agreement was developed by the Smiths and Steve, with clear and specific requirements for Steve to complete.

The meeting was about to wrap-up. Carol and I could sense the energy of the group was diminishing, and I offered the possibility of a follow-up meeting to check out how things were going and to determine if any adjustments might need to be made in the restitution agreement. All agreed that this would be a good idea.

Then Steve looked at Carol and me saying, "I think that would be a good idea. Could we have the meeting at my house?" He then looked at the Smiths and said, "You know, I'm not a burglar. I mean, what I did was wrong, I broke into your house, but I'm not some criminal. I'd like you to come to my house and meet my wife and my little baby."

If I had a valid research instrument that could clearly visualize and measure energy, I would guess with tremendous confidence that you would have seen enormously thick, toxic, tense, closed energy at the beginning of our meeting. Then you would also have seen that transform over the two hour period to the ending. The energy became light, open, receptive and full of connection among people. As we walked out to the parking lot, Steve and the Smiths forgot about Carol and me. They were totally engaged in conversation, with the Smiths asking Steve about his daughter, her name, age, and interests. They were just talking like neighbors, like human beings. And eventually Steve got in the car with us and we headed home.

Losing Her Eyesight as a Young Woman:
The Physical Nature of Forgiveness

C hris grew up as a young girl in a small rural town in the Midwest. She was diagnosed with diabetes as a child but never let her illness interfere or bog her down. She still partied with her friends, and her love of life was contagious. As she turned thirteen Chris began having some vision problems. Her doctor seemed to think it was manageable. In the midst of her high school activities and busy life, the vision problems worsened. Over time, it became clear that her diabetes was triggering the vision loss. In a couple of months, she was blind. Chris was full of rage. Questions plagued her. Why me? How could this happen? How can I hang out with my friends when I can't even see them? Her anger consumed her. She became depressed and withdrawn.

After many months of trying to live with her blindness full of poisonous anger, Chris finally realized that her rage was taking away the energy she needed to live, to feel meaning in her life, and to connect with her friends and family. Talking it out with others did not work for Chris. She directly faced the reality of her blindness, felt the pain and grief, and after many tears, Chris let those feelings go. She found serenity in accepting that which she could not change, no longer focusing on the past. Rather, her energy was now focused on what she could change, the energy and attitude she brought to the new normal she was now developing in her life.

Without using the word, she forgave her body and her God for failing her. Chris said this experience of forgiveness was powerful; it felt like something left her body, as if she physically released the poisonous anger and pain. She felt lighter. Her energy and passion for life returned. Chris re-connected with friends, deepened her relationship with her mom, and found new meaning in life. Within several months she had a new boyfriend. Since this experience, Chris has shared her story with many others, giving them the gifts of her humor, strength, and hope.

The emotional energy beneath the verbal language of the conflict and trauma that Chris faced was powerful. She found peace but not from problem solving and extensive verbal processing of the issues with a therapist or friend. Instead, Chris moved toward a greater sense of peace by finding her own way of letting go of the anger and expectations. This release had a profound effect on her mind, body, and spirit. Chris was able to connect with her own inner resilience and strength. She was able to largely disarm the life consuming emotional power behind the trauma of becoming blind at such a young age and direct her energy toward healing, growth, and new challenges. Despite her blindness, Chris danced with the ebb and flow of the energy she felt in her mind, body, and spirit.

Driving While Black:
Facing Compounding Conflicts

Micah is an African American man from Pittsburgh. From his earliest years, he was exposed to the harsh reality of racism. He remembers being a frequent target of racial slurs and being passed over in job opportunities because he was black. Micah grew up in an alcoholic family with a tremendous amount of conflict. He had a passion for music and eventually played in a band. Music became his way of coping with his own conflict and trauma. When he played music, he was happy.

Much later in Micah's life, he became trained as a family therapist, an organizational consultant, and restorative justice practitioner. In addition to the conflicts of the past, whether it was being stopped for "driving while Black" in White neighborhoods, or periodic racial taunts, new conflicts continued to emerge. Micah would have a hard time with these battles.

And yet, Micah often spoke to me about how he realized he had choices. He could hold on to the powerfully negative energy of the conflicts, both past and present, and the sense of violation and injustice he felt, or he could make choices to consciously disconnect himself from that toxic, life consuming energy. The wounds would still be there, but perhaps their power could be neutralized.

While Micah was making healthy decisions regarding his out-look on life, he experienced a number of very severe illnesses. Threats to his health and well-being presented a different kind of conflict with very real traumatic implications. Through major heart bypass surgery, organ failure, and dialysis, Micah had new choices to make about the conflicts and trauma in his life. He could focus on all of the cumulative conflicts, the racism he has lived with, and the severe illnesses he was now faced with. He could feel sorry for himself and angry at the world for the hand he'd been dealt. Or he could accept the situation as his current reality.

Micah often used the term "energy" in reference to his emo-tions, his life choices, his physical body, his spiritual needs, and his relationships. He realized that if he hung onto the anger, it would zap him of the vital energy he needed to heal. Even in the midst of his significant health challenges, in addition to the prior conflicts he carried with him, Micah made the choice to control the only thing he had power to: his own energy, the choices he made, and the possibility of finding peace within himself.

In the midst of all of these major physical problems --his body was failing him and he was on partial disability --Micah was laid off from his work. The agency had previously led him to believe that his was a very secure job and that the agency was going to be quite accommodating to his physical disability, allowing him to work on a part-time basis. And yet, with little notice, he found out he was going to be laid off. Here he was a single male, with major health problems and no regular income. He wondered to himself if his firing was about race. He had received very mixed messages about his performance from an essentially White leadership team.

Micah felt anger kick in, that righteous sense of, "This is wrong. This is unfair. This is racist."

Part of him wanted to get a lawyer. And yet, as he reflected upon this more and struggled daily with his own health and wellness, he recognized again that the only thing he had the power to change was the attitude and energy he brought to the decisions before him. Micah recognized that he needed every ounce of his physical, emotional, and spiritual energy to be focused on the healing of his mind, body and spirit. In the end, Micah made a conscious choice to not sue the agency and to redirect his energy to his own healing.

Micah's story, again, represents the powerful impact of directly facing conflicts, even when they are multifaceted. He was able to make peace with conflict by recognizing its energetic dimensions, far beneath the spoken words. Micah took the path of peace within, embracing the energy of life.

Meeting Her Dad's Killer:
Forgiving and Freedom

C arol was fifteen when her father was brutally murdered at the insurance agency that he managed in the Deep South. Her dad was having an affair with one of his employees. The woman's husband, Jake, learned of the affair, felt betrayed, was overcome by anger and hatred, purchased a gun, and went to where his wife worked. Jake barged into his wife's office, dragged her over to the office of Carol's dad and killed him, firing his pistol six times at point blank range. Ultimately, Jake was caught, convicted and received a very long prison sentence.

Twenty-two years later Carol contacted me and asked if I and the Center for Restorative Justice & Peacemaking at the University of Minnesota could help her with meeting the man in prison who killed her father so long ago. Jake had already served seventeen years in prison and he was now eligible for parole. When Carol and her family heard of this, they became consumed with intense feelings of vulnerability, anger and uncertainty. They decided to speak at the hearing, and the offender was not approved for release. Carol contacted me shortly after the parole hearing and expressed her strong inner sense of needing to meet Jake even though the rest of her family had no interest whatsoever.

From the beginning it was clear that Carol was yearning to find peace within herself; hoping this might finally end the unresolved anger, the toxic energy, she had frequently directed to her husband and children. Making sure that Jake would not be released at the next parole hearing and holding onto her anger at him for killing her dad wasn't helping her emotional or physical well-being.

Over the following nine months several meetings were held with Carol and Jake separately, to explain the program, listen to their needs, clarify expectations, and to prepare them for the eventual meeting, very similar to the process I told you about in the first chapter with Karen and Peter.

Jake, the offender, felt tremendous remorse for what he had done and was willing, though scared, to meet with Carol. During the separate meetings with Jake, it became clear he both yearned to meet with Carol and was also afraid to do so. The day of the face-to-face meeting came. It lasted six hours. During that entire time, my co-facilitator and I spoke less than ten minutes, yet we both were totally emotionally present, and available to hold the sacred space that emerged. Our role had shifted from that of facilitating an emotional meeting to bearing witness to the strength, resilience, and compassion of two deeply wounded individuals.

My co-facilitator and I practiced mindfulness through centering and breath work both during the preparation and in the dialogue so that we were able to keep our egos and voices out of the way of the dialogue and allow Carol and Jake's strength and wisdom to emerge and flow as needed.

After very brief opening comments by us as facilitators, we entered an extended period of silence as Carol sobbed and tried to find her voice to tell her story. We did not intervene to move the process along. Instead, we remained silent until she was able to speak. After nearly two minutes, Carol found her voice and her story of trauma, loss, and yearning for healing flowed out with strength and clarity.

Carol said she felt truly empowered by the mere fact that she was sitting next to this person who had changed her life. She said she had thought about this moment for years but didn't know how or when it would happen.

"I was dealing with the fact that this is a truth - that this is not something that you can lock away," Carol said. "This person has a life to live. We shared a common experience."

Jake offered his story of what happened, how it had affected his life, and the enormous shame he felt. They continued to share deeper layers of their stories, interspersed with lingering questions from both. Carol and Jake told us later that the energy of our presence, the non-verbal language of our spirit, was vital to the process being safe and respectful of her and Jake's needs and abilities.

After six hours and shortly before the session ended, Carol looked directly at Jake and told him she forgave him for killing her father. She hadn't planned to do this.

"As the meeting with Jake was nearly over I realized this was my moment -- this was the time," she said. "All of a sudden I heard the words I forgive you coming out of my mouth."

Carol spoke of how she no longer was willing to stay connected to these crippling feelings that had weighed her down for so long. She made it clear later that this forgiveness was about freeing herself from the pain she had carried with her for more than twenty years, letting go of toxic energy that had been infecting her entire life and well-being.

Carol had never indicated in our many months of preparation that forgiveness was an issue she was struggling with, nor did we raise the issue. When she and her husband came to the prison for the dialogue with Jake, she had no plan whatsoever to offer forgiveness. Yet in the powerful moment of confronting her greatest fear, Carol said she felt within her soul that "this is the moment to free myself."

Carol and Jake both indicated the enormous effect this encounter had on their lives. Carol spoke of how meeting Jake was like going through a fire that burned away her pain and allowed the seeds of healing to take root in her life. She said before meeting Jake, she carried the pain of her father's death like an ever-present large backpack. After their meeting, the pain is more like a small fanny-pack, still present but very manageable and in no way claiming her life energy and spirit. Jake reported a sense of release and cleansing, as if his spirit was set free as well.

Carol told me that upon arriving at her home after the meeting in prison with Jake, she laid on her bed and, "I took a deep big breath…it just kept going in and in and deeper. I didn't realize had constricted my chest and my entire life had been for so many years."

A year later I again checked in with Carol.

"Meeting the source of my fear and anger, Jake, truly freed my spirit. It was difficult and exhausting, yet I have no regrets for having done this. Today my life is brighter and lighter, full of hope and passion for each moment with my husband and children and friends."

Meeting Her Attacker:
Forgiveness as Instinct

Until the fall of 1995, Jackie Millar was a single mom who worked as a meeting planner, and enjoyed nature photography. But that November changed all that. Jackie was visiting a friend outside of Madison, Wisconsin. While her friend was trimming trees on his farm, Jackie took a nap. When she awoke to a noise in the garage, she came upon two troubled teenagers who were about to steal her car. They violently corralled her into the house, instructed her to lie on the ground, and shot her in the back of the head. Later the teens bought dinner at McDonalds with Jackie's money and burned her car.

Jackie Millar survived. She was rushed to the hospital and given a two percent chance to live. Though she survived the shooting, she still had to struggle through months of painful rehabilitation. Seizures that plagued her recovery were so painful that she was almost driven to suicide.

Today, it's still a cause for celebration when she is able to tie her shoes on the first try. Her speech comes haltingly. She walks with a cane, and her face droops slightly on one side as if she had a stroke.

Now in her fifties, Jackie travels around the country telling her story as a crime victim. She talks to audiences large and small – she even appeared on Oprah. Her message is simple: She forgave those who attempted to murder her, and it's made all the difference.

"I think I would be nuts if I hadn't forgave," Jackie said. She forgave them as soon as they were arrested, "so that I could get on with my life."

Two years after the crime she visited Craig Sussek, the young man who had pulled the trigger. Jackie said her motivations were two-fold: she wanted to tell him that she forgave him, and find out why he did it.

Jackie offered the young man her hand during their interview. Eventually he grasped her hand and told his story while they both looked at the floor.

"It was as if it was my son telling me this horrible thing he had done," she said.

Finding out why may never be possible. Sussek has a hard time explaining his actions when she met him, except to say that he had suffered abuse as a young man. He said he still didn't understand how his actions escalated to that level. Sussek said he had not seen a future for himself before the shooting. Jackie Millar's offer of forgiveness allowed him to feel unconditional love – a foreign emotion in Sussek's life until then.

Jackie expressed her need to let go. Seeing, touching, and talking with her attacker somehow made this possible. But Jackie's feelings about the young men who nearly murdered her are complicated. Though she has forgiven her attackers, she isn't sure what she would say at their parole hearings.

"If they are clearly better than before, and are willing to be men, I think I would talk for them. If not, I think I would talk against them."

Jackie Millar regularly speaks to audiences of lawyers, juvenile delinquents, students, and police officers. It's what gives her story and her pain meaning. When people hear her, it sinks in deep. Sometimes after she speaks, she hugs audience members.

Jackie's story isn't without pain and regret. She's legally blind so she wasn't able to actually see her son graduate from college or get married. Her life still is a struggle day-to-day.

"What you see before you is God's will," she said, adding, "I live my life through Him, that is all I know...He gave me my life back, so I do Him a small little favor – go out and talk to boys, policeman, district attorneys, to all."

Jackie is such an inspirational presence and a wounded, humble woman so loaded with life wisdom and strength. I frequently invite her to speak in my university classes or seminars in the community. If you are feeling sympathy for all of what Jackie has lived through, let it go now! Let Jackie's loving energy flow deep within your soul. Accept this precious gift. Jackie embodies the true energy of compassion, forgiveness, healing, and a wonderful sense of humor and passion for life.

Note: Real names and actual events are described in this very public story that has appeared in newspapers, on evening TV news and even on The Oprah Winfrey Show.

Meeting Her Son's Killer:
The Healing Power of Forgiveness

Tasha is African American and lives in the inner city of a mid-sized city on the west coast. Her son was killed in a mistaken gang incident at a party one evening – shot in the chest three times at close range. When Tasha learned of her son's death, she was numb, in disbelief. She couldn't eat for a week. For months she lay awake at night waiting for him to come home. It was a level of sorrow and anger beyond what she could ever have imagined.

The young man who killed her son was caught, convicted, and sentenced to prison. Tasha's experience in the court system worsened her sense of victimization. The judge mistook her for the perpetrators mother in the sentencing hearing—as if she was just another faceless gang-banger's mother. She felt powerless, unable to have her voice heard.

In the early years following the death of her only child, Tasha would often times speak to other groups and individuals about her pain, telling her story of loss. She found this helpful as part of her own healing process. In those early years Tasha could not have conceived of ever wanting to meet the man who was arrested and imprisoned in a correctional facility. She was in the midst of her over-whelming grief. During that time she looked for support from various groups, but did not find enough relief from her pain. For ten years she suffered almost entirely alone, with her Christianity as one of her few solaces.

Twelve years later, after so much cumulative grief, loss, and pain, she had finally healed enough to begin to think about starting her own group, to help others like her and to help herself. She was introduced to the restorative justice program coordinator from the Department of Corrections (DOC). Although the purpose of the meeting was to discuss how he might support her work, it turned out the meeting had a much larger purpose.

Part of this person's work with restorative justice at the DOC included assisting with correspondence between people in prison and the people they had harmed. He asked Tasha if she ever thought about writing to Isaac, the teenager who was now a man serving twenty years in prison for murdering her son.

Tasha was quiet.

Was this something she wanted? Was she capable? Tasha thought to herself.

This question led to more conversations, and Tasha ultimately decided that she not only wanted to write to Isaac, but she also wanted to meet him in prison.

She realized that, "if I was going to help others heal, I first needed to know deep in my heart that I had truly done my own healing—I needed to prove to myself that I had forgiven Isaac."

Tasha understood that her healing process at that point in her life's journey was directly linked to facing the very source of the conflict and trauma she experienced in the murder of her son. She requested to participate in a restorative justice program called Victim Offender Dialogue. At first the offender refused, but after a second request he agreed to meet with her. Again, many months of separate preparation for her and for the man in prison who killed her son took place. Five meetings were held with each; a great deal of deep listening and gentle guidance occurred.

Tasha wanted to know why this young man killed her son. She wanted to know why he had changed his name after the fact. Tasha never had the chance to tell this young man directly how her son's murder had affected her. The judge had not allowed her to face him in court when she gave her victim impact statement. Meeting him in prison would now provide this opportunity.

After they had talked for over an hour, Tasha told the young man who had taken her son away from her that she had forgiven him.

"I am letting you go cause I need to free myself. I want you to become the man that God has put you on this earth to be."

After four hours of meeting with Isaac, Tasha spoke of how as she left the prison and walked outside she felt a kind of energy moving through her, from the bottom of her toes, a force moving within her, moving up through her legs, through her abdomen, up through her chest, and then just flowing out the top of her head.

"I knew that all the animosity, all the hatred, all the anger and bitterness – it had left. I've never felt anything like that in my life," she said, "I felt 50 pounds lighter."

What happened as a result of this process, she can only describe as a miraculous healing.

"I was free," she said.

Over the years, I have seen similar responses as Tasha's with so many others I have worked with as a facilitator of victim-offender dialogue. For many, the most frightening event they can imagine turns out to be a gift. The dialogue with her son's killer was a gift of awakening that brought Tasha closer to living in the moment, to appreciating the precious and fragile gift of life. She was again reminded that in the final analysis we are all children of God, we are all human beings, and we all carry many wounds. That doesn't excuse people who have done bad things, but it certainly puts what happened into a very different context; a context that has the potential for freeing our souls.

After this experience, Tasha began to invite others to join her vision and began organizing in the name of forgiveness. Today, her work in this realm continues to evolve. She is the founder of a healing group for parents whose children have been murdered and for those whose children have committed murder.

"Because we can understand each other in a way that no one else can," Tasha explains.

The group holds an annual prayer walk, where they walk through their inner city community and pray for peace and for an end to the violence; an important celebration of life event. Tasha also gives community presentations across the country, inviting others to witness the power of healing through forgiveness.

"Our goal is to teach people how to use that vision to heal in their own lives," the mother avows.

Post 9/11 Hatred
Toward Muslims:
Personal and Public Reconciliation

A few hours after watching the live footage of the 9/11 terrorist attacks on television, Christopher Younce, a 33-year-old in Eugene, Oregon, went to his phone book, looked up the Islamic Cultural Center in his area, and made a call.

The director of the Center, Tamman Adi who is a prominent leader of the local Muslim community answered the phone. Younce raged and spewed profanities.

Adi tried to converse with the caller saying, "Maybe we should wait to see who really did it."

Younce didn't want to listen to reason and continued his tirade, even threatening death to all Muslims. Tamman Adi hung up, but Younce called back and this time left a very incriminating message on the answering machine.

Later, Adi described feeling frozen with fear and uncertainty. His and his wife's fears of retaliation were palpable. In the Middle

East, where he came from, death threats are taken very seriously. They were left feeling, "like sitting ducks."

Tamman Adi immediately contacted the Human Rights Commission to enlist their help and protection. They were able to trace the call and identify the caller - Younce was arrested, and released after a short time.

Soon after, the District Attorney's office noted that Christopher Younce lived in the Bethel neighborhood, so instead of going to court he could go in front of a new Community Accountability Board, which was part of a local restorative justice initiative. The assistant to the DA was a strong restorative justice advocate and had worked with the Community Accountability Board on previous cases. She referred the case to the Restorative Justice Program of Community Mediation Services.

Two other important factors helped bring the case to a restorative justice meeting: first, the once belligerent caller told the prosecuting attorney of his intent to apologize and make amends, and; second, the Muslim leader and his wife expressed willingness to speak with the man who had threatened them. If the restorative justice conference was unsuccessful, the district attorney's office made it clear to the Adis that they would continue with full prosecution.

The facilitator of this conference, Ted Lewis, held several separate meetings with Younce and the Adis. During these meetings Lewis and two other co-mediators listened to how this event affected their lives, learned of their needs, and introduced them to how the eventual face-to-face meeting in the presence of other concerned community members would unfold. Younce indicated during the preparation meetings that he had acted out of rage, yelling into the phone, wanting to blame and to scare the Muslim leader. The news had run stories implicating Osama Bin Laden that morning, Younce said, and he equated all Arab Muslims with terrorist extremists. Afterwards, he felt badly about what he had done. He was under a lot of scrutiny after the local press picked up the story and the incident was on television and in print, even making national headlines. The Associated Press headline on September 13th, read "Eugene man charged with threatening Muslims."

Younce said he had a long history of anger problems, which had reached crisis levels after the death of his son and a recent job loss. Although he had felt the need for counseling, he had never taken that step. Just hours prior to meeting with the mediators, however, he had finally called a counselor. Opening the phone book to find the number, he turned to the same page where he had found the number for the mosque. He had a jolt of insight.

"I went to the very page looking for help that I went to in order to create the problem," he explained.

Younce learned about restorative justice and its focus on repairing the harm done to specific victims. He wanted to apologize in person to the Muslim leader and his family, and do whatever was asked of him to make things right. He wanted the opportunity to show them that he was a better man than his actions suggested.

"I'd like a peaceful solution," he said.

A week later, Lewis and the other two mediators met with the victims, the Adis, a husband and wife who ran the Islamic cultural center. The director of the local Human Rights Commission joined them. Two points emerged from this meeting: first, the couple had been traumatically affected by the hate call, and second, they were committed to finding some way of mending the harm. After responding sensitively to the first concern, listening respectfully to the victims' experience of harm, the mediators were able to address the couple's second concern, building trust in the potential for a peaceful resolution.

At the heart of the husband's concerns was motive.

"Why did he do it to us?" Adi explained that he was a scientist, and needed to account for the causes behind actions. He wanted to meet with the offender and hear him say why he did it and, hopefully, why he wouldn't do it again. He could even envision an embrace after exchanging words of reconciliation.

The couple and the mediators also discussed the current political climate and the way it was affecting all Muslims. Newspapers were reporting new hate crimes every day. The nation was at war and Muslim Americans were being mistaken for the enemy. For the Adis, the death threat changed their lives overnight.

A police officer was assigned to protect them; he would open their mail, check their car, and accompany them to speaking engagements.

Mrs. Adi, like many Muslim women fearing retaliation, stopped wearing the *hijab,* the traditional scarf Muslim women wear around their head and neck.

A boy approached their daughter at her high school and said, "We should round up all the Muslims and shoot them."

A simple phone call would rattle them, as it could be another threat. Yet in the midst of this frightening climate, scores of local people were calling to express their support and solidarity with the Adi's.

Throughout this intake meeting, the victims repeatedly turned the conversation to the topic of negative stereotypes fostered by popular media. As a means of helping to restore some balance in media portrayal of the Muslim experience, it was agreed that this meeting could be shared with the public in some way.

The first joint meeting was set for October tenth, nearly one full month after the tragedy. Twelve community members of the accountability board attended the meeting. The prosecuting attorney, the assigned police officer, a representative from the Human Rights Commission, and two others who helped to launch the board — the assistant district attorney and a probation officer - also took part. Lewis served as lead facilitator. He made sure that the victim and offender parties, along with their support people, could sit in separate areas accompanied by a staff person familiar to them. This was meant to ease the stress of entering a room bustling with people before the conference.

There was a lot of emotional tension in the room over the next two hours. Introductory statements by Lewis acknowledged the unique aspects of this case in light of the September 11th attacks. Noting that harm was caused by destructive words, he highlighted the importance of using constructive words in a restorative justice process that sought to repair these harms.

Younce apologized early on, but the Adis doubted his sincerity. They didn't feel like he was answering their questions squarely. Younce had to convince the Adis and the community board that he meant what he said. If he didn't, the prosecuting attorney was prepared to file criminal charges against him.

The community members had important things to say to both parties. They made several empathetic statements to the Adi's and conveyed to Younce that they were there to support his process of accountability and reintegration into his community. Younce, though appreciative of the process, was overwhelmed by all of their questions. The pressure to say the right thing was almost too much.

At one point, a community member pointed out that Tamman Adi was not able to make eye contact with the offender, though his wife was able. Adi acknowledged that this was so. It seemed that he came into this joint meeting feeling more fearful, more vulnerable than ever.

In spite of the limited success of the first meeting, everyone agreed to meet again in order to work toward a better sense of resolution. During the following weeks, Lewis checked in with the parties by phone, and was encouraged to learn that everyone was still invested in a positive resolution to the case.

The Adis needed to spend time going over the questions they wanted answered, and firming up their requests for restitution. They were still struggling with questions like:

"Did he act alone or as a member of a racist group?"

"Was this a first-time racist act, or part of an ongoing pattern?"

"What was in his mind between the time of seeing the news and picking up the phone?"

The Adis needed to hear Younce state why he did it, and why he wouldn't do it again. They also wanted very much to know whether negative stereotypes in the news media played a role in the offense. They were trying to figure out for themselves why they were under attack.

When the parties came together for the second meeting, they again waited in separate rooms while the community members took needed time to debrief from the previous meeting and to get oriented for the follow-up session. Lewis proposed the agenda for the two-hour meeting in which the parties would attempt to complete the discussion of harm and motives during the first hour, and move into the resolution stage in the second hour.

The court reporter from the region's primary newspaper came to this meeting, which was part of the effort to engage the public. Lewis explained that the reporter was there "off the record," but would likely be involved in follow-up interviews and future coverage.

The community members opened with a brief discussion of community expectations for neighborhood residents, and the impact of the crime on the community. Younce then began by providing an update on his progress with counseling, with his family and relatives, and with his job. He mentioned that he had told his employer about the whole situation, which impressed the victims. Most importantly he brought up the death of his infant son, helping the Adis understand the very real, human suffering behind Younce's misdirected rage.

Tamman Adi responded, addressing a string of questions to the offender. Younce did his best to answer, covering much of the same ground he had covered in the first meeting. Only this time, Adi was better able to take in the answers offered.

"I'm satisfied with what I have heard," he said in response. "I think we can move forward."

A palpable shift of energy took place in the room. The prevailing tensions were exchanged for a lighter, more optimistic mood.

After a short break the group began to discuss options for restitution. The Adis asked for a public letter of apology to the Muslim community. They also wanted Younce to attend two upcoming lectures on the religion of Islam. After further discussion, three more agreements were added: Younce would cooperate in news coverage of the case, commit to continue his counseling, and (at the request of one community member) speak to teens in juvenile detention about his experience. The assistant District Attorney created a written document that was signed by all parties.

At one point the concern was raised that Younce's new job might be jeopardized by the press coverage. Adi said that if it came to that he would personally talk to the employer to help the offender keep his job. Younce was moved by this, but simply

80

said that he was willing to accept any and all consequences for his actions.

At the close of the meeting, Tamman Adi unexpectedly reached across the table to shake Younce's hand. It was a moving gesture that spoke eloquently of the progress the two parties had made. Once the agreement was signed, those present got up and began shaking hands with one another in good spirits, buoyed by the sense of relief and reconciliation in the room.

Christopher Younce did attend two lectures on Islam. At the first, Tamman Adi met him at the door. They shook hands, and the court reporter was present with his camera. Inside, Younce sat next to Tamman's wife. He later spoke to Lewis by phone saying that he had enjoyed being there, had learned a lot, and was motivated to attend additional lectures on his own. He also submitted his apology letter, which was printed on the editorial page of the Register-Guard.

A number of factors contributed to a successful resolution of this conflict including a remorseful offender who was willing to make things right, and a victim committed to peaceful dialogue. The community had an established program for addressing conflict restoratively, and collaboration between the agencies providing services to victim and offender helped pave the way for a face-to-face meeting. Finally, once the parties were brought together, they committed to work through the tense emotions toward eventual resolution.

In the midst of the volatile cultural climate following the September 11th terrorist attacks, the case involving Younce and the Adis embodied the courageous journey from hatred to healing.

It offered hope for peaceful, creative solutions to conflicts rising out of misguided rage and racial prejudice. It allowed a grieving Oregon community to play a cathartic role in responding to a local hate crime that had great symbolic meaning in the context of a national tragedy. Their story and others like it, shows how community reconciliation and personal growth can emerge from some of our most painful life experiences.

Note: Real names and actual events are described in this very public story that has appeared in several newspaper stories.

Facing Neo-Nazi Hatred Toward Jews:
Moving Beyond Words

Rabbi Benjamin arrived at his office Friday morning a few minutes after nine. He felt a cool winter breeze and within minutes found the entire front window of the temple shattered, with several bullet holes in the interior wall.

"Thank God no one was in the building at the time of this shooting."

An increasing sense of vulnerability, fear, and anger pulsated through every fiber of his being. It was as though the entire weight of the historical trauma of the Jewish people rested on his shoulders. Yes, there had been previous incidents of anti-Semitism in this small mid-western community, but nothing of this magnitude had ever occurred.

Rabbi Benjamin immediately called the police and then other leaders in the congregation. After extensive investigation and a number of pieces of evidence, the police determined that this act of vandalism, a hate crime, was likely the responsibility of a local cell of young Neo-Nazis that they had been watching.

Within ten days, the police had arrested and charged three young men, two of whom had extensive prior arrests related to hate crimes. These two secured a well-known defense attorney and pled not guilty, hoping to avoid conviction, since they believed the prosecutors had only circumstantial evidence; however, both were eventually convicted and sentenced to prison.

The third young man arrested was seventeen. It was Alex's first trouble with the law. The prosecutors consulted with Rabbi Benjamin and referred the young man to a local restorative justice program that would allow interested members of the congregation to meet him, express their anger, talk about the historical trauma of the Jewish people, and get answers to many questions. Most did not want to meet this young Neo-Nazi. For many, to even walk into the same room and talk with this "monster" was to recognize his humanity. It disrespected the painful legacy of their people. Some had family members who were killed in the gas chambers of the Nazi regime in Germany during the past century.

Ultimately, Rabbi Benjamin and twenty-three other members of the congregation agreed to meet Alex. Who was he? How could he do such a terroristic hate crime? What about his parents? Does he know anything at all about the history and trauma of the Jewish people? This meeting would only happen if all, including this young Neo-Nazi, were willing. It was voluntary. After much thought and in recognition that a far more harsh punishment could await him, Alex agreed to meet Rabbi Benjamin and the others.

A mediator from the local restorative justice program met with the congregation's members to help prepare them for this meeting with Alex. He then met with Alex a week later to also prepare him for the meeting. All involved were very anxious about the eventual meeting, not knowing what to expect. The mediator, Rick, met several more times with the two sides over the next two weeks. Finally, they seemed ready and willing to proceed.

The meeting was convened in a conference room at a local community center. Chairs were set in a large circle. Rabbi Benjamin and the members of the congregation arrived first and were seated. Ten minutes later Alex arrived and entered the room with the mediator's assistant. The tension and anxiety in the room was palpable.

The energy of both anger and vulnerability was intense. Rick opened the meeting with a moment of silence. He then offered a few brief comments, explaining how the circle process works. Rick would ask a series of questions, beginning with introductions, and a talking stick would be passed clockwise around the circle. Only the person who received the talking stick was to have the opportunity to speak or pass it on if they had nothing to say. All others were to listen to the person with the talking stick, without comments or questions. Later on, the talking stick would be put aside and cross talk could occur, with specific questions of each other being answered. Any plan to repair the harm caused by Alex would need to be agreed upon by all. It would then be written and presented to the prosecutors as a plan to hold Alex accountable. If successfully completed, Alex would avoid a prison sentence, although several weekends in the local jail might be required based on the recommendations of all those present in the circle.

The talking stick was passed to Rabbi Benjamin who sat on the left of Rick. The Rabbi held the piece in silence, in deep reflection. After several minutes, he began to speak of the hatred and terror the Jewish people have experienced throughout history. Rabbi Benjamin went into specific details about the death of his mother in the gas chambers of the Nazis during the Holocaust and the impact of this trauma on his life. Fifteen minutes later he passed the talking stick to the next person. Other members of the congregation expressed similar themes, including anger at the horror of such a hate crime.

When the talking stick finally came to Alex he was visibly nervous and unable to look directly at others. After several minutes he began to speak of his difficulty in fully understanding the impact of what he did until this meeting. Alex's parents and uncle taught him from birth about white power and the honor of protecting his race from Jews and Blacks. Until now Alex actually thought that what he had done was honorable.

This was extremely hard for the Rabbi and the others to hear, but they listened.

Alex began to slowly express the emotional energy of shame for his behavior, not yet the much desired words of apology. When he was finished, the talking stick again went around the circle, responding to another invitation for comments from Rick. The comments now offered by Rabbi Benjamin and many, but not all, of the congregational members present had a different energy. Voice tones were more subdued, even difficult to hear at times. The most vocally angry and loud participant before Alex spoke now offered comments that many would find hard to believe.

"Before, I thought you were a monster. Having heard your story I now see a frightened young kid who was acting out his truth, the misguided truth of your parents. You haven't said the words, but I feel you expressing a genuine sense of shame for your behavior."

Rick was gently nodding as this comment was offered. Seven more members of the synagogue made comments about what they were experiencing, witnessing a scared young kid facing the real human impact of his actions.

Rick invited comments about developing a plan to repair the harm caused by Alex, to the extent this was realistically possible. Rabbi Benjamin stated the cost of repairing the window and wall with the bullet holes must be the starting point. All nodded, including Alex. Many other ideas were presented for repairing the harm. Finally all agreed that in addition to financial restitution for repairing the damage, Alex would attend three lectures on the history and beliefs of Judaism, as well as attend two Friday evening services at the synagogue, to be followed by a meal with the Rabbi and other interested persons.

Alex nervously agreed to this plan while also thinking it might have been easier to just spend time in jail watching TV. The prosecutors accepted this plan. Upon completing these responsibilities over the next 6 months, Alex was invited into the home of the Rabbi, along with several of the most initially angry participants. They shared a meal together and reflected on what all had experienced in this restorative justice circle process. Rabbi Benjamin and several others now consider Alex to be part of their family, an outcome no one could ever have anticipated.

All who participated in this process danced with the energy of severe conflict and trauma, sometimes expressing their strong views and sometimes listening. Words were necessary and helpful, but oftentimes lacking. Yet the emotional presence and vulnerability of all involved parties led to transformation and healing, to a renewed sense of compassion, connection, and reconciliation.

Israel and Palestine:
Recognizing the Humanity
in Your Enemy and Yourself

I t was a rainy afternoon in January, when Sarah, a young Israeli Jew, left her house in northern Israel to go to a nearby village to pick up her infant son at his daycare center. As she slowed down to turn safely to the access road of the neighboring community, two Palestinian teenagers approached her car and signaled her to stop. The older of the young men, Mohammed, asked her to take him and his friend with her to the next village, which just so happened to be the same place to which she was traveling. Feeling pity for the boys standing in the cold rain without proper attire, Sarah told them to get in the back.

Sarah continued driving, but as she glanced at them through the rearview mirror, she saw that they each had knives in their hands. Sarah next felt the touch of the cold metal of Mohammed's blade against her throat, a feeling that continues to haunt her.

She asked the boys through her panic, "What is it that you want? What's going on?"

Mohammed spoke to her in a threatening tone of voice telling her to pull over to the shoulder and stop the car. She was in a state of shock but continued driving until she saw a car approaching from the opposite direction. When the car came closer, she signaled it as if she was in distress. While all this was happening, she was driving with one hand on the steering wheel trying to drive straight and the other hand grasped Mohammed's hand that held the knife on her throat.

Suddenly, Sarah stopped the car, loosened her grip on Mohammed's hand, threw off her seat belt, and jumped from the car in order to save her life. The boys also jumped out of the car as it began to roll down an embankment. When Sarah saw the boys escaping, she used her body to try to stop the car from rolling down but without success. Sarah was in a state of shock, and her body was trembling. The driver of the approaching car was someone that she knew from the local village and he called the police. Once he knew that the police were on their way, he picked up her child from the daycare center, and brought Sarah's infant son to her.

This is a story about a foiled robbery. Nobody was seriously injured, save Sarah's car, but the violence and trauma of that rainy January afternoon stayed with Sarah for the next year. The Palestinian boys, Mohammed, fifteen, and his friend Sami, fourteen – both Israeli citizens -- robbed Sarah of her sense of safety and security. Their eventual reconciliation shines a light on what is possible through restorative justice despite obstacles of political strife, and strained cultural relations.

That same day Sarah returned home, but her life had changed. The question that plagued her was what could have happened to her children if she was injured or killed. Sarah felt guilty for taking a chance on the boys. She knew she had put herself in danger, as well as her family. Sarah even thought about the terrible things that could have happened to the boys and their families had she lost control of the car and they had been injured or killed. Her mind was consumed by thoughts of so much pain, sorrow, and loss for herself, her family and the boys.

Over the next year, Sarah's life was filled with feelings of vulnerability, terror and death. The toxic energy of these feelings seemed to take over her entire life like a cancer metastasizing in her soul. It was hard for her to be with her Arab friends, even though this had been a normal part of her life before the attack. She found it difficult to function at home, and her three children also showed signs of distress.

Over the course of the next year, she avoided passing through Arab villages, something that she didn't previously think about. She quit her job and avoided projects that dealt with the Arab community. Every time she heard Arabic she would feel a chill in her body and feel as if she was reliving the trauma. Relationships with her Arab friends became increasingly strained. She knew that they weren't guilty, but emotions overwhelmed her. Seeing a therapist helped a little, but only a little.

The lives of the boys also changed since their attempted carjacking. It was their first brush with the justice system and it scared them. Mohammed and Sami were interrogated and detained in a juvenile facility for over two weeks. Afterwards, they were under partial house arrest enabling them only to attend school. Israeli authorities charged them with attempted robbery and conspiracy to commit a felony. The weight of being separated from their families during detention, the anger of their families toward them after the fact led them to despair after their arrest. Their friends didn't look at them the same way. At school, their crime was condemned and their alienation became so acute that they changed schools.

Their families suffered, too. Mohammed's father had a heart attack when he heard about the incident. His father felt ashamed and desperately wanted to contact the victim in order to remedy the situation. For her part, Sarah didn't want anything to do with the boys or their families. Sami's father also was immensely embarrassed by his son's actions. He had raised thirteen children, and his son's crime hurt his good name and the name of the family.

The boys and their families expressed a strong desire and willingness to correct the damage that they had done and meet with the victim. They tried to contact Sarah around the time of the crime, and in different ways, they tried to convey their desire for "sulha," a traditional Arab peacemaking process and ritual to resolve a conflict.

The juvenile probation officer for the boys consulted with the restorative justice unit of the Juvenile Probation Services to see if they could arrange a meeting between the parties. The boys' probation officer believed a face-to-face meeting between Mohammed and Sami and Sarah, and their families, could offer an opportunity for the type of direct and respectful dialogue that would restore relations in both families, as well as their communities, and start to repair the harm that occurred.

In separate meetings with the families of Mohammed and Sami, the mediator sensed that both boys had a sincere regret for what they did and true desire for reconciliation. Their parents condemned their children's behavior and also spoke of the heavy burden they carried since the day of the crime. The parents accepted responsibility for the acts of their children and the boys were extremely embarrassed in front of their parents for what they had done.

When the mediator called Sarah, she described her emotional state and her many reservations about meeting with the boys. In the end, Sarah said she was willing to meet with Mohammed and Sami, and their families, but she wanted to do so with members of her family and community. Sarah and the mediator resolved to convene a community conference. The mediator contacted representatives of the Jewish and Arab/Palestinian community, including the mayor of the village where the boys lived in an effort to understand the larger context of the crime.

Over the next few months, Sarah wondered if it would be worth the trouble. Despite her fears and concerns about meeting Mohammed and Sami, as she learned more about the program Sarah decided to definitely go ahead with the restorative process. A total of six preparatory meetings were conducted separately with the victim, the offenders, and their families.

A year after the crime occurred, the mediator brought the offenders and their families together with Sarah and members of her family for a community conference. Sarah's therapist and the boys' probation officer also came.

When the mediation finally began, the atmosphere was filled with mistrust. The mediator explained the ground rules, and all agreed to participate. The mediator briefly restated the crime in the context of the political climate following the October 2000 "Intifada," the Palestinian non-violent resistance movement against the Israeli occupation of the West Bank and the Gaza, and praised the participants for their courage to participate in mediation.

Sarah recounted the story of the crime – feeling the knife against her throat, and her fear that she would be just another victim of Arab terrorism against Israel. She remembered her entire life flashed before her.

Were they going to kill her?

Would she ever see her children and husband again?

On paper the crime was robbery, but for Sarah it was an act of terrorism. The boys and their parents nodded as they listened to her words.

When she was done talking, her eleven-year-old son looked directly into the eyes of Mohammed and Sami and told them that they had hurt his mother very badly. He said that he could forgive them but he would never forget how their behavior affected his mother. Her brother told them that she had offered them a ride, and they had preyed upon her kindness.

Mohammed and Sami accepted responsibility for the crime when it was their turn to talk. Mohammed struggled to look up from the floor at Sarah as he talked. He said that he and Sami had watched a violent movie, which inspired them to rob her. Mohammed said that he had no real intention of physically hurting Sarah. He wanted money. He expressed sorrow and deep regret and said that he hadn't considered the real-life consequences of his actions until he heard Sarah's story.

Sami said that he didn't mean to harm Sarah. The younger of the two brothers said that he was afraid of her and the justice system. Sami also expressed deep regret and asked for forgiveness from Sarah and her family. The parents of the boys spoke about the painful feelings they had and expressed empathy for the suffering of the victim and her family. They said they also felt terrible suffering.

After an hour, the room began to warm up. There was a definite shift in the energy. The two and a half hour mediation process allowed the parties to hear from each other how this event affected their lives. They were able to relate to each other as human beings albeit from different cultures, not simply as "victims" and "offenders." The energy and tone of the meeting allowed the parties to speak directly about the injuries to parent-child relationships, education, and neighborly relations between Jews and Arabs.

When Sarah had first entered the room and saw the backs of Mohammed and Sami she actually felt the urge to hurt them. As the mediation slowly unfolded the energy of tension and awkwardness began to shift to a feeling of more openness to listen to each other and speak their truth. Sarah and her family eventually expressed understanding and compassion toward the boys and their families, even the hope that this meeting would affect their lives in a positive way. Sarah and her husband spoke about the boys as if they were their own children.

For Sarah the meeting with Mohammed and Sami gave her an opportunity to re-establish a sense of control and self-confidence in her life. She said she was able to start to better understand the crime and even empathize with the boys. Somehow she was able to stop blaming herself. Sarah's telling the boys' and their families of her fear and anger was actually part of the process of healing. The restorative justice process fulfilled her need to be in a safe place, emotionally and physically, to talk about the impact of this traumatic event in her life and the life of her family, many of whom were present.

For Mohammed and Sami, and their families, this meeting fulfilled their need to directly face what occurred and to take responsibility for repairing the harm caused, in whatever way possible. It also distanced the boys from the criminal subculture by reintegrating them into the community and renewing the trust that they had a place in society. The boys were given an opportunity to take responsibility in an active way towards the victim and towards Sarah's community. Sarah acknowledged that the boys had also suffered, and they understood that their behavior had hurt her as well as her family and community. Mohammed and Sami, and their families expressed willingness to do all they could to heal the wounds their actions had caused.

The meeting ended with an agreement written by the participants, which was later accepted by the juvenile court in lieu of a conviction. At the end of the three and half hour mediation session, all the participants expressed feelings of satisfaction and relief that the process gave them a way of directly facing the conflict, hearing and acknowledging the suffering of each other, and planting the seeds of further reconciliation and healing between Jews and Arab/Palestinians in Israel.

During my subsequent visits to Israel and Palestine I twice spoke with Sarah about the impact of the restorative justice process, the community conference. Each time she confirmed how this conference had a powerful effect on her healing. The second conversation with Sarah occurred six years after the meeting with the boys and their families.

As this second interview began, Sarah paused. Watching her, it was as if she was going back to that time and reliving the event. Sarah spoke of the terror on that cold January afternoon. It amazed Sarah that she had the poise to stay focused and escape unharmed. It had taken all she had – leaving her feeling disconnected and vulnerable when she made it to safety.

Sarah remembered the intense terror and insecurity she felt for a long time, affecting all areas of her life and family. Every little thing seemed to set her off. Sarah's absolute desperation and yearning for healing drove her to meet Mohammed and Sami, and their families.

Sarah said that each time she tells her story to someone, even during this conversation, another layer of release and healing occurs.

"Going back into the pain, the wound, was necessary to find healing from the inside out." Sarah said that in directly facing the source of her conflict and trauma – Sami and Mohammed -- she found her voice and reclaimed her power. "I was now talking to the boys, they listened, and without a knife at my throat. It gave me a lot of strength. It shifted the energy from being a victim to a survivor."

It was difficult for Sarah to hear the story of Mohammed, the boy who held the blade to her throat. He had seemed so self-assured and confident. Yet as she listened more she could see and even connect with the little boy behind the self-assured exterior. As Sami told his story of what occurred and why, he seemed more vulnerable. Sarah felt pity toward both young boys. Yes, they could have killed her. Yet, they were children.

"Everything was silent in my family," Sarah said.

Six years later, Sarah spoke of how meeting Mohammed and Sami and their families changed that, releasing the pent-up bad emotional energy.

"I came out of the meeting feeling stronger, with an increased connection to my husband, my son, and my brother."

Sarah talked about how she believed the event came into her life for a purpose.

"I'm very grateful that this happened. It totally changed my life. It was a gift that shook me out of the bland busyness and fear of my prior life and pushed me into looking at who I really am and what is the meaning of my life."

Today Sarah feels a higher level of spiritual power within her, a new freedom, and the absence of constant fear and worry.

"I never spoke the words of forgiveness, yet I felt its presence. Forgiveness is a releasing of the anger and hurt, of freeing yourself from this bad energy, of recognizing the humanity and wounded-ness of those who have hurt you."

As our conversation came to an end, I asked Sarah, "After all these years, is there a word or two that captures the overall impact of the meeting with Mohammed and Sami, and their families?"

Sarah responded, "A true blessing!"

Sarah's story provides a clear example of the ability of a restorative justice dialogue process to foster accountability and healing between individuals, even while factions of their societies are engaged in a low-intensity war. Had the victim and offenders pursued traditional court-imposed consequences, they would have missed a precious opportunity. Sarah, Mohammed, Sami, and their families reconciled with each other on a person-to-person level. Their ability to do so bodes well for future relations between Israelis and Palestinians as they attempt to rebuild their relationships, even in the current absence of a negotiated final peace agreement, which will surely come at some point. The restorative dialogue experience of these participants has the potential of being offered on a far wider basis and as a bridge toward greater understanding and tolerance among all diverse populations in the region.

IRA Terrorist Meets a Victim:
Redefining Friendship

In the early 1980s the Irish Republican Army (IRA) decided to escalate their tactics of resistance against what they perceived as the oppressive and inhumane British rule of their community in Northern Ireland. Up until this point, all of their operations, or what the British would call 'terroristic acts,' were within Northern Ireland and aimed primarily at, what they would call *legitimate targets*; English officials, people representing the formal English government, whether they be politicians or law enforcement or military people. Yet they felt their goal of freeing the impoverished and oppressed Catholic minority in Northern Ireland and trying to link it to the Republic of Ireland was not being achieved. As a military tactic, they believed they had to bring the conflict, the violence, right into the heart of England, so that the English could feel the threat, and therefore react to it in ways that they believed would be favorable to the IRA's goals.

Patrick McGee grew up as a working class Catholic. He speaks of how he grew up as a pacifist, not believing in violence. But as the years went by, and he saw the oppression that his people, the Catholic minority of Northern Ireland, were experiencing under British rule, he was drawn into the resistance movement. He joined the Irish Republican Army as a way of helping his community, his people. Patrick gained a lot of respect within the resistance movement, or what the English would call 'the terrorist movement' of the IRA. He was found to be very efficient and trustworthy in the military operations that he was assigned by the IRA as a paramilitary organization.

When the IRA decided to escalate the conflict and bring it onto English turf they selected Patrick McGee as the person to implement their plan. Through the intelligence work of the IRA they were not only aware of the annual conference of the Tory government under Margaret Thatcher, convening in the Brighton Hotel in Southern England, they were also able to obtain information on what rooms would be assigned to various political officials, including Margaret Thatcher, as the head of the government.

The plan of the IRA was to strike at the heart of the British government, to literally bring it down. The annual conference would include all, literally all, of the government officials and many others. Patrick travelled into England and to the Brighton Hotel several weeks before the event. He cased out the place; he rented a room that their intelligence informed him was directly under where Margaret Thatcher would be staying. He planted a bomb in the cabinet beneath the sink in a way that could not be detected easily. And he had a timing device for the bomb to detonate during a specific time when it was extremely likely that the government officials would be in their rooms in the evening. Patrick returned to Northern Ireland, having completed his assignment for this military operation.

Several weeks later the annual conference of the Tory government of England was convened with a great deal of hoopla and media attention, including speeches by all the key politicians. On the second day, in the evening, when nearly everyone was in their rooms, the bomb went off. It tore apart much of the Brighton Hotel, blew out the floors at several levels. As it turns out, Margaret Thatcher was not in the room above where the bomb was planted; they had changed that at the last minute.

The operation did not have the full military impact that they had planned, and yet it did kill seven people and injured many, many others, and created a level of terror within English society that they had not known for a long time. The British government realized that the IRA's campaign was being significantly escalated and they prepared with heightened security measures throughout England, protecting other government sites and potential targets.

An intensive police investigation occurred over many months. Eventually Patrick McGee was identified, arrested, convicted, and sentenced to a very long prison stay. While he was there, Patrick did a great deal of reading and actually obtained a Ph.D. in English literature. Prisons that housed both the Catholic paramilitary groups and the Protestant paramilitary groups, separately of course, were essentially like little self-ruled communities within the confines of a prison. They were not one's typical environment of just being locked in and out of the cell. So Patrick made the best of his incarceration, tried to learn more, and tried to grow from this experience.

Over the many decades of the contemporary conflict between Catholics and Protestants in Ireland, there were periodic, formal, direct and indirect attempts to negotiate a peace. In 1996, President Bill Clinton became involved – in the background but in a very important way – in supporting a new initiative that appeared to be very promising to help form a new shared government of Northern Ireland, trying to bring both political and military organizations to the table. To move from bullets to ballots in a democratic fashion. To share governance of Northern Ireland, while still being connected to Britain. And yet, if the democratic majority of Northern Ireland chose to declare independence from England, that would be allowed, as well.

This peace making process was consummated on Good Friday in 1996. As part of the Good Friday Agreement there was a decommissioning of weapons on both sides and there was an amnesty agreement negotiated in which many political prisoners on both sides were freed and allowed to go back to their communities. Patrick McGee was one of those who were freed, after serving seventeen years in prison.

During the Brighton bombing in the 1980s, Sir Anthony Barry was one of those killed. He was a very high ranking official in the Tory government. His daughter, Jo Barry, contrary to Patrick, grew up in upper class Protestant society in England. She was a cousin of the late Princess Diana. Upon learning that Patrick McGee had been released under the Good Friday agreement, Jo began a journey of trying to make contact with Patrick MaGee, to find meaning in what had occurred, trying to understand why he and the IRA killed her father and the grandfather of her children.

Even before the release of Patrick MaGee from prison, Jo had begun a quest of making contact with the IRA through third parties that were trusted by the IRA. Arrangements were made for her to go blindfolded into the Catholic community in Northern Ireland, to meet some of these IRA leaders. Jo was able to listen to them about their political concerns, their goals, why they believed violence was the only way to free themselves. She began getting a glimpse of why her father was targeted and killed. Eventually Jo realized that she really wanted to meet Patrick McGee.

Jo contacted a friend of mine who lives in Dublin, Anne, and who is very connected to the Catholic community and some of the paramilitary groups. Jo asked my friend if she could be a go-between and contact Patrick McGee and see if he was willing to meet her. Anne agreed. Patrick was a bit reluctant, but eventually decided he would try it. Arrangements were made for the two of them to meet at my friend's home, with no press awareness, and no facilitator even present.

When I've talked with Jo and Patrick on several occasions, they both speak about how powerful this initial meeting was. They later met several other times. The BBC television network in Northern Ireland documented these meetings.

The encounter between Jo Barry and Patrick McGee gave Jo some answers to many questions she had, but most importantly, it allowed her to speak of the tremendous impact her father's death had on her family. She heard Patrick's version of what happened. She also learned about Patrick, who he was, what led him to this, and the impact it has now had on his life. And yet there were also points that were very difficult for her to deal with. Even after all these meetings, Patrick could never express any remorse about his choice to become involved in the IRA; though he felt very bad and apologized for the death of Jo's father, who was still, in Patrick's mind, collateral damage in a military operation. He could never disown his allegiance to and involvement in the cause of the IRA, and that bothered Jo.

Following a number of meetings, Patrick and Jo now openly speak about how their relationship has developed. They are not simply meeting as victim and former combatant anymore. Jo openly speaks about how they have become friends who care about each other. They've met each other's families. Not friends in the common sense of the word, but friends in the sense of realizing the woundedness in both of them, and their search for meaning. Their paths had crossed in a way that had a traumatic and transformative impact on both of their lives.

Jo and Patrick have come together to speak their truth to the broader Irish community and the international community. They are committed to the power of restorative and transformative dialogue to humanize conflict, to shift the energy from violence and hostility to rebuilding communities and relationships. Their story is an example of how far beneath the words of conflict and trauma is a powerful emotional energy that can connect people and transform their lives, even as full verbal clarity and truth about what really happened can never be obtained.

Note: Actual names and circumstances are presented in this story that has been documented in various newspapers and a British Broadcasting Company documentary.

Political Violence in South Africa:
Replacing Revenge with Relationship

In the early 1990s, an American Fulbright Scholar, Amy Biehl, was conducting research in South Africa in support of the freedom movement. Nelson Mandela was an inspirational leader to Amy, as she witnessed the yearning for freedom of Black Africans in a country dominated and controlled in brutal, fascist manner by a small White Christian minority government under their racist policy of apartheid. She continued to build relationships with different South Africans, visiting numerous communities and gaining a deeper understanding of the overall conflict.

Amy was out in one of the townships on a Saturday evening, walking to a friend's house. She had no idea that the Pan African Congress (PAC), a more radical branch of the resistance movement than the dominant African National Congress (ANC), had chosen to escalate tactics. Similar to the IRA in Northern Ireland, the PAC believed that their voices were not being heard; hence, they needed to bring the conflict and action right into the white community. Prior to this, political, government and military officials were the targets. Now they concluded that any white citizen was a target.

As Amy was walking down the road, Mongezi Manqina and several of his comrades in the radical group were returning from a rally. Manqina and his friends came toward her, wrestled her to the ground, and stabbed her multiple times in the chest. Amy died alone in the dusty streets of the township. They had no idea that Amy was not their enemy. She was not a part of the apartheid government. She was an outspoken critic of the government and a full supporter of the liberation movement. They had no idea, and it didn't matter to them; she was white, thus she was a legitimate target in their minds.

Eventually the goals of the liberation movement were achieved. The white apartheid movement could no longer rule the country because of increasing resistance and the reaction of the international community. Apartheid leaders agreed to open democratic elections.

Nelson Mandela, the former imprisoned revolutionary leader, was elected the first president of the new South Africa. Oftentimes in scenarios like this, those coming into power view it as a payback time – a chance to punish those who were their former oppressors. Many within the liberation movement in South Africa certainly assumed this would occur, but President Mandela set an entirely different tone. He declared to his country and the international community that a new day had come. He said it was time to build a multi-racial South Africa; it was not a time for blood revenge. Mandela set up a nation-wide process called the Truth and Reconciliation Commission; hearings that would provide opportunities for both white and black people -- who were harmed and those who committed the brutalities -- to tell their stories. Victims would be able to recount their trauma, and perpetrators would be able to own up to what they had done. Ultimately if the commission believed they were telling the truth, perpetrators of the violence could be eventually granted amnesty. The whole focus of the Truth and

Reconciliation process was to foster a spirit of forgiveness and healing within a deeply conflicted and wounded country.

Four of the men who were involved in the killing of Amy Biehl, including Manqina Mongezi, appeared before the commission. Linda Biehl and her husband came from America to be part of the Truth and Reconciliation process, to witness what was happening. In my conversations with Linda Biehl and Mongezi of South Africa, it was clear that appearing for the Truth and Reconciliation process was not only a part of the national healing of South Africa; it was also part of the healing within the individuals who testified. And yet it also became very clear that for many like the Biehls, far more was needed. A more intimate, smaller group format was needed.

The Truth and Reconciliation Commission hearings were large public events with a quasi-legal tone. Linda Biehl and her husband needed more than this large public event and were eventually able to meet Mongezi face to face. Their many questions about what actually happened were answered. The Biehls were able to speak of their love for their precious daughter and the pain they felt over her loss. Mongezi told the story of his choice to join the resistance and to fight for the freedom of his people. He expressed his sorrow for killing their daughter, having no awareness at the time that she was a supporter of the resistance movement. They talked numerous times and over the years developed a connection of respect and concern for each other, despite the tragic event that brought them together, the killing of Amy. Mongezi recognized that Linda Biehl was not simply the mother of a legitimate target of the resistance movement, and Linda Biehl recognized that Mongezi was not some terrorist monster.

Like the IRA militant Patrick MaGee, Mongezi believed his acts were part of a larger struggle that was right.

"South Africa is free today because of the bloodshed," he said.

But he also regretted hurting her.

"I realize it was bad," he said. "I asked Amy's parents to forgive me."

Following the death of her husband from illness, Linda Biehl established the Amy Biehl Foundation in South Africa to promote constructive youth activities that can be part of fostering healing within the nation. To this day, she remains connected with Mongezi, whom she hired to work at the Amy Biehl foundation.

Many years later at a conference in the Midwest, I invited them to attend and tell their story. Mongezi and Linda again spoke of the tremendous healing that had occurred within their lives through meeting each other, through directly facing the trauma and violence that had occurred.

It would be hard to find a clearer act of public policy and presidential leadership in any country that shifted the energy within an entire nation, moving it from the quest for revenge and retaliation to one of healing and reconciliation.

As good as that sounds, one should have no illusions. The Truth and Reconciliation Commission fell far short of many of its planned objectives. Few representatives of the apartheid government ever appeared before the commission. Virtually none of the high-level policy makers of the apartheid system of racial oppression and control appeared before the Truth and Reconciliation process. Far more from the Black South African resistance community appeared than whites. None of the hoped for financial restitutions were ever actually paid to individual families that lost loved ones.

Yet on an energetic level they succeeded enormously. As incomplete as it was, the Truth and Reconciliation Commission's process provided a safe setting for huge amounts of the accumulated toxic energy to be released in a public way that began to cleanse the soul of the nation. It helped pave the way for building a new multi-racial South Africa.

<u>Sources</u>
South Africans Apologize to Family of American Victim Wednesday. (1997, July 9)
The New York Times.
Letting Go; Beyond Justice: The Eternal Struggle to Forgive. (2002 May 26) The New York Times.

The Parents Circle
in Israel/Palestine:
Using Mutual Grief as a Path to Peace

Amir Hirshinzon had served the Israeli Army for only three months when he was killed by a suicide bomber at Beit-Lid junction, a crossing from Israel into the Palestinian territories. Amir had been trying to rescue survivors of a suicide bomb when a second bomber blew himself up. Amir's father Ronni heard the news from his younger son.

As a young man, Ronni had served in the Six Days War of 1967. His eldest son Amir believed he was following in his father's example to serve as a paratrooper. Ronni had told him to be careful.

"A good soldier is a live soldier," he said.

Serving in the military is obligatory in Israel for all young men, and women. When Ronni's younger son, Elad, enlisted, Ronni convinced him to serve at the Army radio station so as to avoid direct combat. Elad did, but when his best friend was killed in a conflict, Elad couldn't take it and he shot himself in his radio station office. Two sons dead.

In his pain, Ronni co-founded the Parents Circle-Families Forum in an effort to make peace between Israelis and Palestinians through dialogue. Half of its several hundred members are Palestinian and the other half is Israeli. The prerequisite of membership is that you have lost a loved one in the conflict. The group brings together Palestinian families with Israeli families for weekend forums where bereaved families tell their story to the 'other side.' In the process they form relationships.

Ghazi Briegieth is Palestinian, who as a young man threw rocks at Israeli tanks. His brother, Yusef, a heavy machinery operator, was killed when he was 31 by an Israeli soldier deemed to have 'psychological problems.' Yusef's wife was left behind to care for the couple's two children.

Ghazi is in his forties now, and has three kids of his own. He named his youngest boy Yusef. He continually talks to his children about the possibility of reconciliation instead of revenge.

One would think the Parents Circle would be welcomed by their mutual governments and communities, but sadly their peacemaking efforts actually come with quite a bit of personal risk. For Ghazi, being a leader in the parents' peace circle means crossing the border into Israel, illegally sometimes, and hoping he is not stopped for traveling without a permit by an Israeli soldier. When Ghazi is at home, his neighbors are suspicious. In Ghazi's community, the most common message given to those who have lost loved ones isn't forgiveness or reconciliation; it's revenge. At one point, he had to procure a letter from then-president Yassar Arafat about his work with the peace circle so as to insulate himself from threats at home.

The Parents Circle-Families Forum is absolutely committed to making peace between the peoples and they see themselves as having a unique voice to do so.

Ronni said, "If we, who paid the highest price possible, can talk to each other, then anyone can."

Aside from the forums, the Parents Circle-Families Forum created a phone service called Hello Shalom/Hello Salaam (Hello Peace) that some thought was doomed to fail because it was so radical. It works like this: an Israeli leaves a message needing to talk, and a Palestinian calls him back, and a Palestinian bereaved family would then be called by an Israeli. In one year, they had over 200,000 calls.

"We need people to, first of all, talk to get out the anger," said Ghazi. "They need to know on the other side there is a voice of peace."

The telephone project was started by accident when a telephone operator connected Natalia Wieseltier, an Israeli, to a Palestinian home in Gaza.

"A man picked up and said I had a wrong number," Natalia told the Guardian paper. "I said who is this, and he called himself Jamal and said he was an Arab living in Gaza. Instead of hanging up I asked him how he was. He said he was very bad, his wife was pregnant and their town was under a curfew, and we ended up talking for about 20 minutes. We weren't making apologies to each other; I wasn't trying to make him feel better. We were just talking as individuals. At the end of the conversation he said he was amazed that Jewish people were able to talk like that. He thought we wanted all Palestinians dead."

Jamal ended up encouraging his brother to call Natalia. Natalia thought the idea of talking to regular people from the other side of the conflict held real promise so she approached the Parents Circle-Families Forum, which has run the program ever since.

Ronni said conversations start off a little heated sometimes but then something else happens.

"There's some shouting and some cursing at first, but then it becomes: Where are you from? How old are you? That's all it takes for people to start communicating, to start humanizing the other side. The crucial thing is to change the perception each side has about the other. Callers realize that the other side is experiencing the same anger and frustration as they feel, and that's a very disarming experience."

Ronni has to cross into Palestine, the occupied territories, illegally to keep the organization going, just as his Palestinian colleagues need to cross into Israel illicitly. He says he and Ghazi talk daily over the telephone, but seeing one another is also important.

In 2002 Ronni crossed over to go with Ghazi to talk with a Palestinian family who had lost a teenage son. Ghazi met him just over the border, on the other side of the army checkpoint. They drove in Ronni's car to the bereaved family's house. The brother of the boy, Mizar Albaniej, greeted the men and invited them in. The family greeted him, and they sat on the families couch and shared a cup of tea. Mohammed Albaniej, the boy's father, said he had worked with a Jewish carpenter back when it was possible to cross into Israel to make one's livelihood.

The boy's mother showed Ronni where soldiers' bullets had left holes in their windows and in the ceiling. She said when she sees a bombing in Israel and watches dead kids being carried away, she thinks of her son.

"Just like others need to live, I need to live."

Ronni told the family how he had lost his sons. Ronni said both sides – Israeli soldiers and Palestinian militants do terrible things. Mizar, the dead boy's brother, asked Ronni why his kids were in the military. Ronni explained that it wasn't about choosing to enlist in the army, if his son didn't go, he would go to jail.

Ronni came to invite them into the group.

"Next week, the Parents Circle-Families Forum is hosting a seminar."

As he leaves, Mizar said he would come.

Ronni still grieves the loss of his children, but this work, this radical people to people diplomacy keeps him going.

He says he doesn't talk about forgiveness, "until they give my son back."

"But I can try," he says pausing, "to reach reconciliation. That's the way to solve the conflict."

Restorative dialogue among enemies is extremely difficult while the conflict is still alive and violent. Feelings of fear and vulnerability are ever present on all sides. The bombs set by Palestinian suicide bombers periodically pierce into the daily routine of Israelis while the Palestinians view the actions of Israel as imposing a state of terrorism on their daily lives.

Participants in the Parents Circle-Family Forum understand at a very personal level the tragically high cost of continuing generational vengefulness. In addition to supporting each other, they speak to groups in many other countries. Robi Damelin, an Israeli activist in the organization, whose son was killed while in the Army reserve by a Palestinian sniper, and Ali Abu Awwad, a former Palestinian revolutionary whose brother was shot and killed by an Israeli soldier, frequently appear together to speak internationally as peace campaigners. Whenever I have been present with Robi and Ali, I can sense a deep shift in the energy between them; a shift that cuts through decades of intense hatred, violence, and revenge that has characterized the conflict in the Middle East; a shift toward a greater understanding of the enormous suffering of both Israelis and Palestinians. It's a shift toward embracing policies that stop the violence and begin the difficult process of peace building through dialogue, mutual recognition, tolerance, respect, and reconciliation.

<u>Sources</u>
Peace on the line. (2004, May 12). The Guardian of London. Retrievedon 2/5/10 from http://www.guardian.co.uk/prius/parttwo/story/0,14195, 1214886,00.html
Another Side of Peace by Ellen Frick and Gretchen Burger.
Encounter Point directed by Ronit Avni. Co-directed by Julia Bach.

The Women of Liberia:
Using Feminine Energy to End a War

Leymah Gbowee and women like her had watched for years as men escalated the violence in the streets and countryside of Liberia in West Africa. The nation's president, Charles Taylor, had armed mere children, who in turn committed unthinkable acts — amputations, torture and rape were commonplace. Warlords who sought Taylor's ouster had resorted to the same tactics. As time went on, the violence only seemed to increase. More and more refugees had fled to the safety of Monrovia, Liberia's capitol city.

As a leader in the Women's Peace Building Network, Gbowee helped bring an end to a civil war in Liberia that had raged for over a decade. Gbowee, a social worker, had found herself fleeing the civil war when her town was attacked. Together with women from her church, she decided to try to stop the violence.

Visiting with mothers in refugee camps, who had seen the worst of the war, Gbowee remembers holding their children and seeing an uncanny resilience.

"I looked into their eyes and even though they had lost everything, they still had hope," she said. "I think that's when I got baptized in the Women's movement."

"I had a dream," Gbowee said. "And it was like a crazy dream, that someone was actually telling me to get the women of the church together to pray for peace."

Lehmah Gbowee observed President Taylor using the churches to rally support for his government. And she saw how warlords, confederated into a group called Liberians United for Reconciliation and Democracy, or LURD, spoke in mosques. Gbowee reached out to Muslim women to join with her in pressuring religious leaders on both sides to oppose the violence.

As the months passed, the violence worsened near the capitol. The Women's Peace Building Network protested daily at the fish market despite ominous threats from Taylor against assembly. As their numbers grew, Taylor eventually could not ignore them. The women read a statement in front of parliament. Their message was simple and did not take sides or make policy statements.

"We are tired of war. We are tired of running. We are tired of begging for bulgur wheat. We are tired of our children being raped. We are now taking this stand, to secure the future of our children because we believe as custodians of society; tomorrow our children will ask us, 'Mama, what was your role during the crisis?' Kindly convey this to the President of Liberia. Thank you."

With this, the women successfully pressured Taylor to attend peace talks in Ghana. They then sought out rebel leaders, and convinced them to attend the talks too. Lehmah Gbowee and other women followed them there to see for themselves how the peace process worked.

After six weeks, the women were getting frustrated. The talks seemed like a vacation sponsored by the international community for Liberia's warring factions, rather than a serious peacemaking effort. The women believed the men were just enjoying the hotels and per diems, so they decided to act again.

They linked arms, and surrounded the hall where the men were meeting. They said the men could not leave until they had signed an agreement even if it took days. When confronted with security guards and asked to disperse, Gbowee threatened to strip if they arrested her. A bold act, as in Africa it's extremely taboo to see a mother naked.

"That was a moment of rage," Gbowee said. "I mean, it's... when you've been disgraced and you've been walked on, when your pride has been just, there is nothing left, when people think they've taken everything from you, you decide you're giving them some of what they thought they'd taken away."

Aware that their actions were still not effective enough, Gbowee and the other women of the Women's Peace Building Network even resolved to withhold sex until the men quit fighting. The men backed down, and returned to negotiations. The women allowed the men to leave that evening but vowed to act again if the two sides did not negotiate in good faith.

Within weeks, the leaders had signed an agreement. Over the next few months, a transitional government was installed, United Nations peacekeepers entered Liberia, and President Taylor fled to Nigeria to live in exile. In 2006, Liberia welcomed its first female president, Ellen Johnson Sirleaf, who won the country's first democratic election in decades.

"What we did was make the Liberian's bold. We stepped out first and did the unimaginable," Gbowee said.

Few were untouched by the violence during the fourteen-year inter-tribal war that killed more than 200,000 Liberians. Gbowee and her fellow activists pushed for reconciliation and peace. They pushed men to disarm, and put their faith in words and agreements rather than guns. Gbowee and her network remain engaged to keep the country moving away from the violence that they believe patriarchy brought.

The actions of Lehmah Gbowee and the Christian and Muslim women of Liberia offer a powerful statement of working with the energy of severe conflict and trauma. They did not rely on research, policy analysis, or the influence of powerful key political players to represent their voice. Instead, they channeled the physical, emotional, and spiritual energy of common but courageous woman to light a fire under the recalcitrant warlords involved in the peacemaking process. Through placement of their physical bodies in strategic locations of non-violent resistance, through withholding sex to their men until genuine negotiation of peace occurred, and through countless other non-violent actions, the women of Liberia became the tipping point that led to a final peace agreement and the election of the first female president on the African continent.

Sources

"Pray the Devil Back to Hell" (June 19,2009). Bill Moyers Journal. Retrieved on 2/5/10 from http://www.pbs.org/moyers/journal/06192009/profile.html.

Pray the Devil Back to Hell Director Gini Reticker (left) and Producer Abigail E. Disney, March 2008.

Cancer:

In Facing Our Greatest Fear,
We Can Find Strength and Healing

Alexa and I had been married twenty-four years. Life was good. We had two beautiful, healthy young daughters. Alexa was now in graduate school for nursing after having supported me during graduate school in prior years. Having found each other during our high school years, Alexa and I connected as true soul mates. Our relationship as spouses and parents was very precious, full of unconditional love, joy, humor, and support through the hard times. And then CANCER came into our lives and shook us to the core of our existence: facing our greatest fear, facing our mortality, and triggering a lifelong journey of awakening. A journey that took us from fear to hope, from vulnerability to strength, from trauma to peace.

It all began in October of 1994. Alexa led a very healthy life, with good diet and exercise. During routine breast self-examination during a shower, Alexa felt some tenderness in her right breast. She watched this over the next couple of weeks. It certainly was not a distinct tumor or lump, but something was different. She went to the doctor and a mammogram was indecisive. Just to be extra careful, an ultrasound was also scheduled.

Again, nothing clearly indicated the presence of cancer. Finally, it was determined that a biopsy from her right breast should be taken. This would provide clear information as to whether or not cancer was present. At this stage, none of her doctors, nor Alexa as a nurse, were concerned that this tenderness in her breast was cancer. Everything indicated it was likely not cancer. For this reason, Alexa felt fine with me leaving for a business trip in Albuquerque, New Mexico, on the day when she would receive the report on the biopsy. I was hesitant to go, but Alexa said there was no need to worry.

Upon arriving at 11:00 pm in my Albuquerque hotel, I called home to Alexa to let her know I arrived and to check on what she found out about the biopsy.

She answered the phone and then said, "Are you sitting down?"

I immediately felt waves of anxiety and fear beginning to pulsate throughout my body. I sat down.

"The doctor said the biopsy indicated I have breast cancer. Further tests are needed to determine how advanced it is."

WHAM! My entire life came to a screeching halt. All of my important life work as a peacemaker, mediator, teacher, speaker, and researcher meant nothing. Every ounce of my energy, my life force, was focused with razor precision on the life threatening reality and trauma our family now faced. First, I told Alexa how precious she is to me and our entire family, how full of anger and sorrow I was at the moment, and yet how confident I was that together we could face this new challenge. Second, I found out that Alexa was not alone. She was with our nineteen-year-old daughter and her boyfriend. Third, I told Alexa I would immediately return, assuming I could catch a red-eye special flight. Fourth, all of my extensive travel and speaking in other states and countries was immediately cancelled for the foreseeable future.

The terror, vulnerability, and pain the reality of cancer initially brought into our lives is beyond words. Our normal sense of time stopped. We had entered an altered state of consciousness. We truly lived in the present moment. Future plans faded. No time existed to think much of the past.

Alexa's initial diagnosis was followed by a surgical removal of her breast that showed the cancer had spread into many lymph nodes, a formal listing of Stage Two cancer. The surgery was followed by a highly toxic and intense regimen of chemotherapy, which caused Alexa to be hospitalized frequently. After the chemotherapy, the quest for finding a new normal, a new routine of life began for all of us. Our life style changed dramatically, integrating an entire new range of activities to foster our spirituality and healing. We integrated a wide range of complementary and alternative healing practices in our lives. Guided imagery, meditation, prayer, healing touch, massage, herbal treatments, acupuncture, diet, and yoga became and remain a vital part of our family's life.

Seven years later a routine doctor's appointment with blood labs determined a significant abnormality. After further testing, Alexa was diagnosed with multiple myeloma, an incurable blood cancer in her bone marrow that likely occurred as a result of the highly toxic chemotherapy she received. While targeting cancer cells, chemotherapy also kills healthy cells.

Breast cancer and the many practices to foster healing within our lives prepared us well for the even worse diagnosis of multiple myeloma. From a western medical perspective there was no known cure for multiple myeloma. Yet we had long since learned there are many practices to foster healing and wellness, to befriend and live with this diagnosis as a chronic, rather than terminal, illness.

Learning the difference between curing and healing has been the foundation of our encounter with cancer. At times, severe illnesses can actually be cured through the marvel of modern medical technology. The disease is eliminated. Most western medical interventions, however, tend to focus on symptom reduction. Healing is focused on how we deal with what we are faced, the energy and attitude that infuses our life. Are we consumed by anger, vulnerability, and fear? Or, have we found a deep sense of contentment and peace regardless of what we faced at this moment of our life's journey, despite periodic moments of anxiety?

As a nurse, Alexa has worked with many patients who were cured of their illness. It was gone. Yet their lives often exuded the energy of anger, fear, and discontent. Similarly, Alexa has worked with many patients who suffered from severe illnesses that no known medical cure was available, yet many of these individuals exuded the energy contentment, joy, humor, and love. Their lives exemplified the presence of deep inner healing; having befriended the condition they are now faced with, even though suffering from an incurable severe illness.

Then skin cancer came into my life. Initially I had been diagnosed with two benign forms of skin cancer. No problem. Then several years later I was diagnosed with melanoma, the most lethal form of skin cancer. Fortunately it was melanoma in situ, contained entirely in one location. Prior to Alexa's encounter with cancer, this diagnosis would have been terrifying to me. Following the many years of learning a wide range of practices to foster healing in Alexa and myself, as well as nurturing a deeper sense of spirituality and healing in our entire family, my response to this diagnosis of melanoma in situ had little emotional power. Inconvenient? Certainly. It is a bit scary with the required surgery and the continual vulnerability to further development of melanoma in other locations because of my health history. But was this a source of intense fear and anxiety? Not at all. We had long since moved out of the world of clinging to, "what ifs."

The wisdom of the serenity prayer was again my guide. I found serenity in accepting that which I could not change in the circumstances that I faced, the cancer that had entered our family's life. I yearned for the courage to change the only thing I could, the energy and attitude I brought to all of what I now faced. In befriending cancer, in accepting its reality in our lives, in letting go of needless energy sapping fear, what used to be our greatest fear truly became a gift of embracing how precious and fragile life is.

Learning to dance with the circular energy of cancer in our lives, from fear to serenity, from sorrow to hope, from vulnerability to strength, and back again to moments of sorrow and even more frequent moments of gratitude and peace has been a gift of awakening that has deeply enriched our lives.

Trusted Neighbor
Violates a Child:
Facing the Enemy Next Door

On a warm summer, late evening in my neighborhood located within the city limits of a mid-size city in the Midwest, my wife and I awoke from sleep because of the smoky sounds and smells of a house fire.

Earlier that day, as I finished my daily jog and reached for the screen door of my front porch, I noticed an inquisitive person at my neighbor's door, writing notes on a pad of paper. This person noticed me noticing him and quickly changed his focus to my front stoop.

"Good morning, I'm a reporter for the local paper. Have you heard about the arrest of your neighbor across the street?" he asked.

"Um, no, I have no idea what you're referring to."

The reporter said, "He was arrested for molesting one of the kids in the neighborhood. You didn't know? He is a fireman in town, and I understand he is very popular with the young kids around here."

He asked me a few more questions but I had little to offer him, so he went on to another neighbor's home.

Wow! How could this have happened?

We live in a very safe neighborhood. He is such a likeable guy. Everyone trusted him, and the kids loved to hang out at his home.

That night at around two in the morning I awoke when I heard a loud crackling sound. I got out of bed, went to the window, and was shocked to see the house across the street on fire. Then I noticed it was actually the garage of Jim, the neighbor who had been arrested. I woke up my wife. We got dressed and then ran across the street to check on our elderly neighbor who lived directly next to the house on fire. Other neighbors also came out of their homes and offered help. Everyone's first reaction at the scene was to think that this was a vigilante crime.

The combination of learning of a local child being molested, the arrest of Jim, and then Jim's garage being on fire led to a tremendous sense of concern, anger, vulnerability, and even disbelief for some. A neighborhood meeting was being organized to talk about this. We met in a neighbor's home. All expressed deep concern for the parents whose child had been violated. All were also given a chance to talk about how this crime affected the neighborhood and their lives. The neighborhood meeting provided a safe place for anger toward Jim to be released. In letting go of the intense anger, for most, a pathway to peace was opened. The anger was transformed into a commitment to building stronger relationships among neighbors, organizing activities, and more effectively living with each other as neighbors.

Gary's Story:
Returning to Native Traditions

My friend, Gary Ten Bear grew up on a Crow reservation in Montana. He is a mixed-blood Native American with Anishinabe as well as Crow roots, and is deeply connected with Lakota communities as well. Gary grew up during a time when the American government authorized what today we would call policies of "ethnic cleansing," as they attempted to strip Native American children of their cultural roots, their language, their ways of being, and their spiritual traditions.

Gary was among those children required to attend Christian boarding schools—to leave their families and their homes. While the Christian missionaries believed they were doing God's work, it is now well known that the actual impact of this forced assimilation, or what today could be called ethnic cleansing, was horrific. Although Gary did not directly experience the physical and sexual abuse that was so rampant in many boarding school settings, he was still traumatized by having Christianity forced upon his life and by being removed from his family and home. Whole communities of people were traumatized by these events, and Gary, like so many others, eventually got deeply involved in drugs and alcohol, and ultimately, crime.

Gary looks back upon his earlier years on the Crow reservation and the forced Christianity with mixed emotions. For much of his life Gary struggled with drinking and other substance abuse, but he's been free from the clutches of alcohol for more than twenty years. The enormous injustice he and his people have experienced, the near destruction of their culture and way of life, can trigger anger in his soul. Yet, he refuses to get stuck in this anger. Every bit of his energy and that of most Native American communities, he believes, needs to be directed toward individual and community healing. Gary recognizes this pain was part of his spiritual path; it's part of what led him to reconnect at a very deep level with his spiritual traditions.

Gary is not only a good friend; he is also my teacher. The wisdom found in Native American culture is an entirely different way of understanding and relating to the precious gift of life we've been given by the Creator. Over the years, as Gary walked the path of recovery, he received guidance from elders within his community, reconnected with the deep spiritual values, and routinely participated in sweat lodges and other Native ceremonies within his community. He is a Sun Dancer and has completed many Sun Dances on the Crow reservation in Montana and on the Lakota Rosebud reservation in South Dakota.

For those of you who are not aware of the Sun Dance ceremony, it represents the ultimate spiritual and physical tests, as you try to reconnect with the essence of life, the sacredness of life, the power of the Creator. The Dance is an ancient ritual in which a group of people, with the support of the larger community, spends a number of days fasting, participating in sweat lodges, and each are eventually tethered to a tree with rope or leather. They dance to and from the tree, as their chests are pierced with dowels inserted in the pierced flesh. Ropes are attached to the dowels connecting them to the sun dance tree. After four prayers are given, the sun dancers will struggle to break free from the tree. After breaking free from the tree, the dangling flesh on the chest is an offering for the people. The sun dancer is taking on the suffering for the people so they will not have to suffer.

Sun Dancing can last for several days. It brings people to the very edge of existence, to becoming one with the Creator. Sun Dancing creates a deep altered state of consciousness where one moves beyond their fear, beyond the initial pain and discomfort, beyond the hunger, and is at a place where they feel the powerful presence of the Creator. Sun Dancing therefor is a very transformative, deeply spiritual event.

For many years, Gary has worked across the country with chemical dependency programs that serve Native Americans. In Alaska, he worked with a program where Native Americans struggling with alcoholism and/or drug abuse are not just given talk therapy, but are also exposed to the old ways of their people. They are in the woods without televisions in very humble cabins. No heat. No water. They chop wood and bring it to the community of others in the program. They bring buckets of water from the river. This approach to chemical dependency treatment not only brings them back to the old ways of living, but also teaches them to be and share with others. Gary reports this has been highly effective with the men he's worked with.

In the spirit of Black Elk, the great Lakota spiritual teacher, Gary deeply believes we are at a time in history where the ancient wisdom of the Red Road, the Native American way, is to be shared and given to the larger global community. To help non-Indians come to grips with the precious gift of Mother Earth, how to treat Mother Earth well, how to treat each other, how to move beyond the ways of violence and material accumulation, and how to reconnect at the deepest spiritual level with the energy of life.

Gary has faced high levels of conflict and trauma throughout his life, beginning in his childhood through the ethnic cleansing policies of the government and continuing into his adulthood as he struggled with chemical abuse; however, he achieved sobriety and was able to reconnect with his own spiritual traditions. Gary represents a glowing example of facing conflict and trauma, and finding peace. The peace Gary found had far less to do with verbal processing and far more to do with connecting to the deep spiritual energy of his people and his way of life.

Note: Gary's real name is used with his permission.

Facing Ultimate Terror:
Reclaiming Your Power

Many years ago Carla experienced ultimate terror. Driving along the highway, she experienced car troubles and had to pull off the road. She lifted up the hood of the engine, looked under it, and realized she didn't have a clue what was going on or how to fix it. Another driver pulled over, parked his car, walked over to Carla, and offered her some assistance, presenting himself as a "Good Samaritan." At first the stranger's presence seemed very kind and friendly and just a welcomed relief. But after twenty to thirty minutes, the energy of the Good Samaritan shifted from friendliness to violence and control.

This man ordered Carla into his car, drove off to a secluded area in the woods, where he knew a cabin was, took her at gunpoint, sexually assaulted her, raped her, stabbed her, and then left her for dead. He left Carla unconscious and bleeding. Many hours later, she awoke and somehow found the strength to crawl more than a mile to a nearby home. She asked the residents for help, and they immediately realized she was badly hurt. They called 911 and triggered the process of her getting emergency care and being taken to a hospital.

In reflecting on this experience, Carla describes how from the very moment she regained consciousness on the gurney in the emergency room she forgave the man who did this. She forgave him not because she was some saintly person and not because she was in denial about what had happened to her. Quite the contrary. Carla knew she was lucky to be alive. She also instinctively knew that every ounce of her energy must go toward her physical, emotional, and spiritual healing, not towards hate or vengefulness. Without all of her energy being focused on recovery, she would never see her husband and her children again. Through forgiving the man who brutally raped and stabbed her, she was releasing the clench he and his actions had on her and her body, and therefore freeing herself to heal. Carla reclaimed her own power lying on the gurney that day.

When I spoke with her about this remarkable event, Carla told me about how she just simply let the terror go. Did not give it another thought. The anger was not engulfing. Oh, there were moments of anger, but each time a negative feeling crept in, she simply let it go, and eventually there was no anger at all. She knew she had to focus her energy on her own healing and her own power, and that's exactly what happened.

Despite being diagnosed by different physicians as having a slim chance of survival, Carla had the will to live. She willed her body to heal - through her own energy and power. Yes, she got excellent medical care, but at a deeper spiritual level she felt compelled to live in order to regain her connection with her husband and her children, and after many months of treatments and physical therapy, Carla recovered.

Carla is blind because of the stab wounds to her face and eyes. Because of the massive trauma she experienced, she will never see again in her life. Yet, this woman exudes the energy of compassion, of wisdom, of living in the present moment, of appreciating, loving, and savoring every moment of life. She recognizes that life is a very precious and fragile gift.

Following her severe victimization, Carla's life was transformed in a huge way. For her, forgiveness was truly an act of freeing herself from the clutches of the trauma and it was not dependent on the actions of the offender who was now in prison. It was a bold choice for healing, meaning, wholeness, and power in her new life. Since this incident, Carla has left her job in retail to become a strong victim's advocate in her state. She was appointed by the governor to head a major victim's initiative. To this date, she remains a passionate advocate of restorative justice, a kind of justice that holds people accountable, but also offers opportunities for all parties to heal and to have the harm repaired as much as is realistically possible.

Carla's story is a powerful example of facing conflict and finding peace. Not getting stuck in the poisonous energy of anger and hatred, but rather releasing it, realizing that in holding on to the anger it will continue to poison you. In Carla's case, she experienced the full power of forgiveness, which is a deep spiritual gift to oneself, an act of freedom. Forgiveness may hopefully help the offender, but it is first and foremost about the person forgiving; letting go of that toxic energy.

Carla believes her life today has more meaning than it did before the trauma of her near-death experience. Her life is far less superficial. She doesn't live on the surface of life. She lives at a deeper level, full of joy, full of happiness, full of meaning, full of the willingness to work with other people who have experienced trauma and severe conflict, but not getting stuck in it in terms of her own stuff or her own history, and encouraging others not to get stuck in the anger and pain of trauma either.

Alisha's Story:
Becoming More than You Are

Alisha's daughter was stalked for many months. The twenty-one-year-old girl became increasingly fearful. One evening after she went to bed, at around two in the morning, an intruder broke into her apartment carrying a large knife. He went into the bedroom, jumped on Alisha's young daughter and tried to rape her. The girl fought back, but Alisha's daughter was stabbed multiple times, and despite her efforts to save herself, she was killed on the scene. The intruder fled the scene.

Eventually the intruder, whose name was Jeff, was arrested, tried in court, convicted, and was given a death sentence. Jeff had a history of violent offenses, including sexual assaults by family members. When I interviewed Alisha several months before Jeff's execution date, and following an eight-hour restorative justice meeting she had with Jeff on death row, referred to as a victim-offender dialogue, she spoke about the following (and I should add that Alisha went through a great deal of intensive preparation with a mediator, as did Jeff, before they ever came together). Alisha talked about how walking into the prison to meet Jeff was surreal. It was beyond something she could even imagine. She talked about how she needed to bring the spirit of her precious daughter to Jeff, so he could realize he killed a precious human being, not just some object.

Jeff talked about how sorry he was for what he did, how ashamed he was for what he did. There were many tears on both parts. After a great deal of time spent sharing how this heinous crime affected their lives, particularly Alisha's family life, they also talked about other concerns related to crime and violence in society.

Alisha described how mid-way through the eight-hour dialogue, which had several breaks, she felt a powerful sensation within her.

"It felt like whoosh, like something just rose from my body. It felt like forty pounds of weight just let go."

She actually used some out-of-body metaphors to talk about what happened. When she was later shown a videotape of her meeting with Jeff, she said to the mediator, "That's not me, I couldn't do that. I'm not capable of speaking like that or listening like that."

Alisha spoke to me about her conflicted feelings about Jeff's pending execution. On the one hand she came from a part of the country where it was religiously and politically acceptable to kill people who are convicted of killing others. On the other hand, in meeting Jeff she realized he is a human being and an exceptionally wounded human with a long history of abuse within his own family, beginning from infancy. There was a part of her that was saddened by the fact that he was simply going to be killed, exterminated for this crime. Alisha planned on attending the execution as a witness. Not in the spirit of cheerleading the death of Jeff, or feeling good about it, but rather, to witness the end of a very painful part of her life and to grieve her daughter's death, as well as to grieve Jeff's.

Now, before I go on to tell you more about what happened at his execution, I want to speak about my conversation with Jeff a week before he was executed. He spoke a great deal about his history, about how he was sexually abused by his mother as a young infant—a fact that is well documented in the court system. He had led a life full of anger and victimizing others in very violent ways. The meeting with Alisha was one of the most powerful, transformative events in his life. In fact, he spoke about how when he looked into Alisha's eyes he did not see an angry, vengeful, righteous mother, but instead the face of God, and he felt the presence of God. He said he saw more of the love of a mother in Alisha's eyes, even toward him, than he ever felt from his own mother.

Well, Jeff certainly did not use the term energy, yet he made reference to experiences that I would categorize as that of dealing with the energy of conflict and trauma. He spoke about how he felt so much at peace. He couldn't fully understand or explain why he did what he did. He couldn't even fathom how they came together and the impact it had on their lives, but he knew and expressed in his own words, a tremendous sense of release. He felt peace at the deepest level, even though within one week the state was going to execute him, terminate his life.

I was not present during the execution, but I spoke with a friend and colleague who served as the mediator and who was asked by Alisha to be present as a support for her. Execution rituals are quite full of a number of activities, which try to make this very barbaric, old practice seem more scientifically and medically appropriate, even religiously so, with clergy present to offer their prayers. Jeff was strapped on a gurney with different IV lines going into his wrists. As he lay on the gurney, the warden asked him if he had any words he wanted to say before he authorized the execution.

Jeff raised his head as much as he could, looked through the glass window that surrounded him and said, "Alisha, I am so sorry for what I've done to you and your family and your daughter. I can never forgive myself. I am so ashamed of what I have done. But I thank you so much for coming in to speak with me. The time we shared together was a very precious moment. It was perhaps the most touching moment in my life. I am so sorry Alisha."

Alisha, without anyone expecting, rose up from her chair, went to the window, and touched it, almost as if she was energetically trying to touch Jeff's extended hand as he stretched it out as much as he could from the gurney.

"Jeff, I forgive you for what you have done. May God be with you," she said with compassion in her voice, not the energy of anger or revenge.

The warden looked at Jeff and asked one last time, "Is there anything else you want to say?"

Jeff began to sing "Amazing Grace," a prearranged signal to the warden that he was ready to be executed.

For most people it's hard to conceive of how a mother could spend eight hours on death row within close proximity, even a foot away from the man who viciously attacked and murdered her precious daughter. There are few rational explanations for what occurred. What clearly did happen was an enormous energetic release of toxic energy, of the emotional pain and suffering that Alisha had been experiencing and the suffering that Jeff had been experiencing in a very different way. Alisha would refer later to this whole experience as a very sacred event in her life. And once again, as with all the other stories, it was precisely in directly facing the conflict in her life, the trauma, not just facing it verbally and in her head, but really energetically facing it in the presence of the person who caused that tremendous harm that she found peace, that she found freedom, that she found the ability to move on with her life and embrace life with a new passion.

Gifts of Awakening

M any gifts of awakening, or blessings, are to be found in each of the many stories shared in this book. While each story is embedded in the life context and journey of the specific people, the wisdom shared is universal. Each one of us can be enriched and empowered by having the courage to embrace and practice this wisdom.

Breathing to Serenity and the Power of Deep Listening

There will inevitably be severe conflicts or traumatic events in our lives that are overwhelming, and we cannot easily free ourselves from their powerful dark clutches. Finding serenity or even embracing the energy of forgiveness may seem a far distant and unrealistic expectation at the moment. We simply have to find a way to breathe through it, a process that can at least de-power the toxic energy with which we are living. The most time-tested practice throughout the ages is working with the power of our breath. While in the midst of frightening and stressful events, being mindful enough to focus on the flow of your breath into your body through slow, deep breathing can bring a sense of peace in the midst of the storm, not resolution or full healing, but peace in the moment.

When dealing with others who are going through conflict or trauma, either with us or in their own lives, listening deeply with our heart as well as our head is a precious gift. Many of us go through life without ever having experienced deep listening.

Letting Go of Your Ego

The ego is a powerful force. We need it for our healthy emotional development and our capacity to create. Yet the power of our ego can consume us and massively distort our perceptions of reality, to feed our illusions of who we are and what really is occurring. As often said, ego stands for "edging God out," living in the illusion that we can totally understand, control, and manipulate reality. Sure we can, but to a far more limited degree than we often believe. Yet so much of life and relationship is truly a mystery. Taming the ego through humbling ourselves, through acknowledging our weaknesses, our limited understanding of what is before us, our likely contributions to the conflict or trauma we are experiencing, is a major pathway to peace.

Embracing Life

Life is such a precious and fragile gift, not to be taken for granted. In the midst of the hardships we are facing, we lose perspective. All of our energy can be focused on the specific conflict or trauma. We forget about the good times. We forget about all we have to be grateful for; those individuals who have brought meaning, joy, and companionship into our life, those who have offered unconditional love despite our many faults, the incredible functioning of our bodies despite limitations we all experience, the awe inspiring beauty of nature, the gift of each breath, and so much more to be grateful for, to cause us to embrace this precious gift of life we have been given. In dealing with traumatic health issues within our own immediate family, my wife and I came to learn the difference between curing and healing, and more importantly, learned how to embrace life, even in the difficult moments.

Are we consumed by anger, vulnerability, and fear? Or, have we found a deep sense of contentment and peace with what we are faced at this moment of our life's journey, despite periodic moments of anxiety? In befriending cancer, in accepting its reality in our lives, in letting go of needless energy sapping fear, what used to be our greatest fear truly became a gift of embracing how precious and fragile life is.

Doing the Unexpected

The most disarming of all actions is to do the unexpected. The power of intense conflict and trauma lessens as we honestly embrace these realities as our new normal for the moment, acknowledge their power in our life, humble ourselves, and engage in actions that are totally unexpected by the source of our troubles. Rather than attacking the person at the root of our angry, listen deeply to their story and invite further release of their story. Let our communication be grounded in the energy of compassion, not self-righteousness. Rather than living in fear of the trauma we are experiencing, accept it as a new opportunity to learn, to grow, and to perhaps find new reservoirs of strength within ourselves, that which we never thought we were capable.

Being present with aggressive verbal and emotional behavior that can lead to violence is not easy. Our fight or flight instinct kicks in. Most of us choose to flee the situation; yet sometimes, we can't. Confronting aggression with our own aggression escalates the conflict and can lead to dire consequences. Confronting aggression by doing the unexpected, by not playing into the energy of the aggressor, by breathing and staying calmly focused changes the dynamic and de-escalates the conflict. In response to aggressive behavior, the energy of calm and compassionate communication grounded in authenticity can often disarm the aggressor, just as I was able to do when faced with a terrifying road rage incident. Think also of what the women of Liberia and Nelson Mandela in South Africa were able to accomplish by doing the unexpected - they changed their own circumstances as well as that of their country and the world.

Facing Compounding Conflicts

Sometimes in life we are faced with the horrific realities of several traumas at once. We may have to deal with multiple deaths within our families, for example, or loss of a job while dealing with an illness, as in Micah's story. When this happens, it is more important than ever to keep our energy as positive and focused as possible. Compounding conflicts bring with them compounding toxic energies. During times like these, we are more susceptible than ever to further physical or emotional sickness. By maintaining our breath and concentrating on embracing even the smallest glimmer of hope, we can fundamentally change our futures. Imagine Nelson Mandela sitting in a jail cell for decades and coming out with this perspective:

"There were many dark moments when my faith in humanity was sorely tested, but I would not and could not give myself up to despair. That way lays defeat and death." We all have the capacity for this sort of strength within us.

Releasing Toxic Energy (Anger, Frustration, Hatred) Toward Your Abuser Can Result in Finding a Path to Healing and Peace

The residue of conflict and traumatic events in our lives can leave us emotionally and physically scarred. It can take on a power that is toxic, a power that distorts our image of others, and our self, a power that can even at times call into question the very meaning of life. The path to healing goes through the healthy release of anger and frustration. To hold onto intense anger, to endlessly engage in self-talk and talk with others about the source of your anger, to ignore the toxic nature of anger, is to create a massive obstacle to healing within yourself and among others. At worst, it can lead to severe stress, significant health problems, broken relationships, ever-increasing bitterness and cynicism, and a loss of meaning and direction in one's life.

When deeply hurt and abused, every fiber in our being often cries out for revenge and harm to the offender. To do anything less would seem to diminish the injustice we have experienced. Yet holding on to intense anger, no matter how justifiable it is, can be like a cancer metastasizing in our soul.

As Bishop Tutu expressed, holding onto anger and bitterness can be like taking a daily dose of rat poison and expecting the rat to die. In the process of holding onto our anger, we are actually giving the person who harmed us far more power over our life. Without denying the terrible abuse that occurred, without necessarily offering forgiveness, we can reclaim our power by letting go of our anger toward the abuser, severing the emotional cord that is continuing to hurt us. In doing so, we are not forgetting what happened or pardoning the offender, but instead choosing the path of freedom.

Like in the case of Jo from England and Patrick of the IRA, Patrick never could bring himself to admit killing Jo's father was wrong, and Jo certainly never forgot what happened, but far beneath the words of conflict and trauma is a powerful emotional energy that can connect people and transform their lives, even as full verbal clarity and truth about what really happened can never be obtained. Learning to release this toxic energy in a safe setting, to let it go, can truly be transformative, opening entirely new and exciting pathways in our life's journey. At best, letting go of the pain and anger can become the engine that drives growth and healing within our lives.

Recognizing the Humanity in Our Enemies & Ourselves: The Physical and Spiritual Miracle that is Forgiveness

The emotional energy beneath the verbal language of conflict and trauma is powerful. We can find peace not only from verbal processing of the issues with a therapist or friend, but also from finding a way to let go of our anger and expectations and, if possible, by forgiving. Forgiveness has proven to have a profound effect on our mind, body, and spirit. Through forgiving, we connect with our own inner resilience and strength. Forgiveness can largely disarm the life consuming emotional power behind trauma, conflict, and/or abuse and directs our energy toward healing, growth, and facing new challenges.

Despite the pain or wrongdoing, forgiveness allows us to dance with the ebb and flow of the energy within our lives. Many people who have gone through the process of forgiving have expressed an innate, almost physical need to let go of their pain and anger toward their offenders, that they couldn't really rest or begin to heal until they forgave, as in both Tasha's and Sarah's stories of forgiving their loved one's murderers.

Forgiveness is not an easy task, but is one that seems to come naturally to humans when we allow ourselves to truly listen to our bodies, minds, and souls and stop listening to the invasive toxic energies such as anger and hatred. As was so eloquently described by Carol, when she spoke of forgiving her father's murderer, forgiveness is like going through a fire that burns away your pain and allows the seeds of healing to take root in your life. Unforgiveness can be like an ever-present large backpack weighing you down on your journey, and through forgiveness the pain transforms into a much smaller fanny-pack, still present but very manageable and in no way claiming your life energy and spirit. Those who are able to forgive report a sense of release and cleansing, as if the spirit is set free, just as Tasha reported that day in prison when she forgave her son's murderer and experienced a total body sensation that left her feeling fifty pounds lighter.

Today, both of these women as well as the woman named Sarah from Israel, who was carjacked by young Palestinian boys, report their experiences of forgiveness as true blessings. These women were able to come to this place of blessing and forgiveness, and so can we all, in the words of Sarah, by "recognizing the humanity and woundedness of those who have hurt you."

Tools for the Journey

In bearing witness to the many stories that I've shared in the previous chapters, our lives can be enriched. These people who have endured severe conflict, or who have been hurt so deeply, can be among our most powerful teachers, providing us with life wisdom. In sharing the journey of those who are directly facing severe conflicts or traumatic events, or as we experience those events in our own lives, there are many practices that can give us strength to be there for others and to be there for ourselves.

These practices can nurture our soul, our body, our whole being. No one approach or practice will necessarily be effective for all people. Some of the practices that I am sharing with you can certainly relate to most people; they come from many different cultural settings and have been practiced throughout the ages.

Meditation

The practice of meditation or other contemplative forms of quieting the mind or being still is powerful. It runs against the very fabric, the very energy, of our warp speed modern culture. And yet, there is clear research evidence showing that regular practice of meditation, in whatever form you find fits best with your culture and your life-context, can yield almost immediate physiological and emotional benefits. Meditation is a way of learning to work with breath, to be comfortable in silence, to engage in a practice that tames our minds, and slows down our minds. It allows us to access the energy of our heart as well as wisdom of the mind.

There are many different forms of mediation, and some of those that practice and teach it can be as rigid and dogmatic as any conventional teacher or clergy person. What I encourage, at least as a starting point, is a relatively generic form of meditation that we can all access and adapt to our life context and culture. What I've shared with you previously about mindfulness is the starting point to developing a meditation practice. Going deeper requires a teacher, oftentimes a group, to practice with for reinforcement. But eventually it can be done alone, if you don't have a group with which to practice.

Even taking just five minutes a day of mindfulness, of centering yourself can become a powerful practice in setting a different tone as you begin the day—so that you don't begin the day with the busy and frantic energy that many of us immediately give into. By taking this time, we can begin the day in a more focused and reflective mode.

Centering and meditation are ways of reclaiming our power, of reconnecting with our wholeness. In my earlier years, I had little time for meditation. I thought it was a distraction, of little use, frankly, a waste of time. I was too much of a social activist, organizing picket lines and demonstrations and involved in prison reform and the civil rights movement and anti-war movements of the past century. Meditation seemed totally useless.

Over the past two decades I've come to a very different point. I've realized it's not a matter of either the contemplative life of one who meditates or the busy life of one who is a social activist. No, it's not an either/or proposition. It's both. Some of my greatest teachers and mentors (such as Gandhi, Martin Luther King, Dorothy Day, Mother Teresa, and many others) are glowing examples of people who integrated some degree of contemplative practice in their lives - tapping into the spiritual energy that is part of all of us, with powerful and effective social action to better the world, and directly addressing widespread injustices and suffering. It's blending contemplative and spiritual energy with the energy and commitment to be of service to others at multiple levels.

As I have practiced daily meditation for more than fifteen years, I have found that I am far more effective, efficient, less stressed and happier if I begin the day with a meditation practice. And as I mentioned in the comments about mindfulness, when you begin meditation, whatever form you're trained in, it's not as if you're going to be in instant bliss. Not at all. Your mind will always wander, because it's full of all these thoughts. Meditation is building on what you can learn from the practice of centering. It's a way of acknowledging those many thoughts, but not fighting them, letting them go, and focusing back on your breath, or focusing on a beautiful place in nature, or focusing on a mantra or some sacred words or a verse from your culture or faith tradition, depending on your life context.

Meditation is not rocket science. It doesn't require a formal degree. It's a relatively simple process to learn. All it takes is sitting in a comfortable position, sitting straight with the back erect, closing the eyes, and breathing slow and deep. When beginning, it can be helpful to breathe in slowly and deep in the belly to the count of eight or ten and then exhaling slowly to the count of eight or ten. You may choose to include a focus on a sacred word or a visualization of a beautiful place in nature that always brings you peace. Learning to use the mantra or the beautiful place in nature as a way of redirecting the energy of the mind, to let go of all of those thoughts, allows that incredible stream of consciousness to pulse through our mind. The goal is to be aware of those thoughts and simply let them pass by, not holding onto any one.

Now this is an over-simplification of meditation, but it is a way of describing the core essence of meditation. Different practices, from different cultural and spiritual traditions, will have a range of techniques and practices. But the core essence of meditation is a way of slowing down the mind, slowing down the ego. It's shifting from the frantic energy of multitasking to a different state of consciousness where one is living more in the present moment, with a heightened sense of awareness.

In meditation, even if there are loud noises in a neighborhood, one can still tune in to the birds chirping or other sounds of nature. And finally, meditation does not have to require being at some retreat, on comfortable cushions and beautiful music in the background. Of course, that's nice if you can do it, and it's a good way of getting recharged, but meditation can occur in any setting. It can occur in even a noisy setting. When my wife and I were in China and learning Qui Gong from Taoist masters, part of what we learned was spiritual Qui Gong, and we practiced a certain type of meditation from their culture. We were on uncomfortable wooden benches, where we sat at the edge of the bench, cutting into our butts. It was a noisy area of Beijing with construction and jackhammers. It was the exact opposite of what I had thought of as a meditative type of environment.

And yet we learned extended periods of meditation, up to an hour, where we could be aware of all those noises, not let them aggravate us, not let our discomfort aggravate us, as the bench was cutting into our butts. But we moved far beyond that. We were truly in an altered state. A beautiful, peaceful, wonderful state, where we were living in the present moment and not taking life or each other for granted.

Working with the Energy of the Body

Working with the energy of the body is an important tool in taking care of ourselves. And there are many forms of, essentially, meditation in motion that can be very helpful, depending on what works for you. For some it can be as conventional as getting into dance, for dance taps into a different energy in us, a very creative energy that takes us away from our thoughts and our minds and our troubles. For others it would be the practice of yoga or tai chi or qui gong or other forms that integrate the contemplative practice of the mind with working with the energy of the body in a beautiful way that brings us into the present moment. For others in can be as conventional as jogging or walking, long walks.

Learning to work with the energy of our bodies can deeply nurture not only our physical bodies but our spiritual, mental, and emotional bodies, as well. Our bodies are largely overlooked in our modern society. We alter them for personal appearances, obviously, but we don't treat them well. We don't give them regular exercise; we don't use the gift of our bodies in the way they're meant to be. So developing a practice of each day, walking a couple miles or jogging around a lake, or doing whatever works for you, going for a bike ride, is very important.

Whether it's meditation (where it brings the mind to peace and nourishes the soul at a deeper spiritual level) or meditation in motion (such as yoga, tai chi, qui gong, or even certain types of dancing), the key issue is regular daily practice.

You may need to learn certain techniques of yoga or tai chi or dancing before beginning your practice, but these are very learnable. And then again, the central issue is practice, practice, practice. Unless we weave them into the rhythm of our lives, unless they become part of the daily flow of our energy, as normal as brushing our teeth or washing our hands, these practices will have very little effect. It might give us a temporary boost, a good feeling, but then we get sucked into the vortex of the busy energy of multitasking that takes us out of the present moment. We reflect on the past, what we did or didn't do. And we're likely projecting on the future, specific plans and goals.

For all of the practices that I will share with you, it's important to realize that their power is not in the periodic practice of the technique. The power is in the daily practice.

Massage

There are many forms of massage that can be incredibly helpful in terms of nurturing our souls and our bodies as we're dealing with the energy of conflict and trauma within ourselves or among other people we're with. Physical massage on a regular basis, perhaps once a month or even more frequently can be very helpful in relieving tensions within our body. There's also energetic massage through Reiki and Healing Touch, which is a type of massage that involves very gentle touch or even above-body work. It can have a powerful effect on our body, mind, and spirit. Energy massage helps release stuck toxic energy and often leads to a very comfortable, peaceful, altered state. There's also a Chinese form of massage called Tui Na, which is a more rigorous, deep massage that has some unique characteristics and can be very helpful. There's a Hawaiian type of massage called Lomi-Lomi, and there are many other types of massage as well.

The point is no one type of massage is a one size fits all. All of massage helps release energetic emotions that get stuck and carried in our muscles and our body. It helps release those tensions so that we feel better.

Guided Imagery

One of the earlier techniques I learned in my own struggle in dealing with my wife being diagnosed with advanced breast cancer was guided imagery. Guided imagery is essentially a form of self-hypnosis. There are many different CDs that you can get to lead you through this. It will usually involve a person with a very gentle voice initially guiding you through progressive muscle relaxation. You could be lying on the floor, in bed, in a comfortable recliner, or on a couch, spread out with your arms at your side, eyes closed. And the voice will guide you to relax each muscle from the tips of your toes to the top of your head. It will then guide you to go to a deeper place. A place where you feel safe. A place that is well known to you where you feel comfort and joy. It's not a prescriptive kind of guidance in most cases. It's trying to guide you into finding a place within your own life experience, your memories. A place where you feel acceptance and comfort. It brings back good energy of the past. And then you will be guided through different ways of dealing with emotional or physical wounds you are carrying.

A series of CDs we have found particularly helpful in our own lives, which was developed by one of the pioneers in the field of guided imagery, is by Dr. Martin Rossman. Particularly for those with exceptionally busy schedules, with little time to engage some of the above self-care practices, guided imagery is a very practical bridge from one's current busy lifestyle to deeper forms of mediation or yoga practice. For many, guided imagery is much easier to integrate into your life. You simply put a CD into your player and then listen to the guide as you are relaxing. For us it was clearly a bridge between our previous, rather conventional lifestyles into a much deeper, richer, more open, and more exciting experience of recognizing the enormous healing powers that are all around us, to be found in all of our different cultural traditions. Healing powers that are far more natural.

More on Guided Imagery

Upon learning of my wife's diagnosis of Stage II breast cancer, a friend offered us some information about guided imagery. My first reaction was to dismiss it. I felt we really didn't need it. We'll pull through this somehow. We were experiencing the pain, the trauma, and the fear this diagnosis brought into our lives. It kept building up, with more power. I finally thought I'd better take a look at guided imagery. My wife and I began practicing guided imagery and it brought us tremendous strength through such a traumatic event.

It was through the daily practice of guided imagery that my wife and I dealt with the conflict and trauma of what we were facing in terms of the reality of cancer entering our lives. It took the power out of the fear, the unknown, the uncertainty, the vulnerability. We certainly had moments of fear, periodic feelings of vulnerability, but it just did not have the power that it used to have.

The truth is, the regular practice of guided imagery was not only tremendously helpful for us in the midst of trauma, in the midst of taming our fears, and in the midst of finding new strength within ourselves for our healing. It also led to a very powerful experience of peace and joy. In fact, I began to ask myself, why do we spend money periodically going on vacation trips when I can feel as much joy and peace imaging my presence in beautiful places in nature through guided imager?. I was also feeling the total absence of all the stress of travel, let alone the cost. Ultimately, guided imagery is a particularly helpful tool in nurturing our soul, in nurturing our bodies, and in nurturing our mind when dealing with the energy of conflict or traumatic events within ourselves and among others.

All of these tools may not fit within your own life context and preference. Yet some can definitely be integrated into your life, your dance with the energy of conflict and trauma that is inevitable in our life's journey. Nearly all communities or regions have resources and trainings on these and other tools. Mindfulness-based Stress Reduction workshops and classes are offered throughout North America and many other countries. These workshops are particularly good in introducing people to the practice of mediation, yoga, and self-care. As you search for training and resources to find tools for the journey in your community, let Google do the work. Simply put in words like: self-care, meditation, massage, yoga, tai chi, guided imagery, and mindfulness-based stress reduction.

Enjoy the journey. Remember, the power of these tools is not in the technical learning of the process in a one-time workshop, retreat, or book. The power to access the wisdom, compassion, and peace within all of us is in practice, practice, and more practice, until it becomes a normal part of our daily routine.

In how we pass each other from storm to center and back – there you'll find the trials and gifts of love.

A Last Word
Dancing With the Energy of Trauma:
Here It Comes Again

In writing the final chapter of this book I was put to the test. While in Italy to give a keynote address at a University conference, I fell down two flights of poorly lit steep stone stairs in an old apartment building. I was still conscious, despite partial amnesia, after having broken my hip and several ribs, along with many bruises and some head trauma. My entire body was shaking and I sensed I was going into shock. I focused on my breath, breathing in slowly and deeply to the count of thirty (far more than I normally would) and the intensity of my fear and pain subsided. I continued focusing on my breath throughout the entire ride in the ambulance and while in the emergency room (with no English being spoken), and I was able to sweat through it and even to find a certain degree of serenity and peace.

My body was broken. The pain and discomfort were intense. Yet the power of working with my breath allowed no space for fear, panic, and anxiety. Buddhism teaches us that pain is real, but suffering is optional.

All of this is captured in the beautiful words of an unknown author:

Peace
It does not mean to be in a place
where there is no noise, trouble, hard work, or even trauma.
It means to be in the midst of these things
and still feel calm in your heart.

A Few Resources to Begin Your Journey

There are numerous excellent books, DVDs, CDs, and websites that are easily available in bookstores and through the internet by conducting Google searches and going to amazon.com. A small sampling of resources is offered here.

Books

A Life of Being, Having, and Doing Enough, by Wayne Muller (2010)

Anam Cara: Spiritual Wisdom From the Celtic World, by John O'Donohue (1997)

Black Elk Speaks: Being the Life Story of a Holy Man of the Oglala Sioux, as told by John G. Neihardt (1979)

Coming to Our Senses: Healing Ourselves and the World Through Mindfulness, by Jon Kabat-Zinn (2005)

Contentment: A Way to True Happiness, by Robert A. Johnson & Jerry M. Ruhl (2000)

Gift of Awakening: Having the Life You Want by Being Present in the Life You Have, by Mark Nepo (2000)

How Then, Shall We Live?: Four Simple Questions That Reveal the Beauty and Meaning of Our Lives, by Wayne Muller (1997)

I Heard God Laughing: Renderings of Hafiz, by Daniel Ladinsky (1996)

Jesus Against Christianity: Reclaiming the Missing Jesus, by Jack Nelson-Pallmeyer (2001)

Living and Dying with Grace: Counsels of Hadrat 'Ali, translated by Thomas Cleary (1995)

Living Buddha, Living Christ, by Thich Nhat Hanh (1995)

Living in Gratitude: A Journey That Will Change Your Life, by Angeles Arrien (2011)

Living Peace: A Spirituality of Contemplation and Action, by John Dear (2001)

Miraculous Living: A Guided Journey in Kabbalah Through the Ten Gates of the Tree of Life, by Rabbi Shomi Labowitz (1996)

Native Wisdom for White Minds: Daily Reflections Inspired by the Native Peoples of the World, by Anne Wilson Schaef (1995)

Pathways to Spirituality & Healing: Embracing Life and Each Other in the Face of Serious Illness, by Alexa and Mark Umbreit (2002)

Peace in Our Lifetime: Insights from the World's Peacemakers, by Susan Skog (2004)

Peace is Every Step: The Path of Mindfulness in Everyday Life, by Thich Nhat Hanh (1991)
Pocketful of Miracles: Prayers, Meditations, and Affirmations to Nurture Your Spirit Every Day of the Year, by Joan Borysenko (1994)

Restorative Justice Dialogue: An Essential Guide for Research and Practice, by Mark Umbreit and Marilyn Peterson Armour (2010).

Sabbath: Restoring the Sacred Rhythm of Rest, by Wayne Muller (1999)

Three Deep Breaths: Finding Power and Purpose in a Stressed-Out World, by Thomas F. Crum (2008).

Twelve Steps to a Compassionate Life, by Karen Armstrong (2010)

Wherever You Go, There You Are: Mindfulness Meditation in Everyday Life, by Jon Kabat-Zinn (2005)

Without Buddha I Could Not be a Christian, by Paul F. Knitter (2009

Links to a Sample of Relevant Web-sites

Belleruth Naparstek
Guided Imagery: A Powerful Tool for Healing Your Emotional
Heart

Center for Spirituality & Healing
Academic Health Center
University of Minnesota
http://www.csh.umn.edu/

Center for Restorative Justice & Peacemaking
School of Social Work
University of Minnesota
http://www.cehd.umn.edu/ssw/rjp/

Jon Kabat-Zinn
Mindfullness-based Stress Reduction
http://www.mindfulnesscds.com/author.html

Restorative Dialogue Learning Module
http://www.csh.umn.edu/wsh/restorativedialogue/index.htm

About the Author

Dr. Mark Umbreit is a Professor and founding Director of the Center for Restorative Justice & Peacemaking at the University of Minnesota, School of Social Work. He serves as a Visiting Professor at the Marquette University Law School in Milwaukee. Dr. Umbreit has also served as a Fellow of the International Centre for Healing and the Law and a Fellow of the Center for Contemplative Practice in Society. He is an internationally recognized practitioner and scholar with more than 40 years of experience as a mediator, peacemaker, trainer, teacher, researcher, and author of eight books and more than 200 other publications in the fields of restorative justice, mediation, spirituality, forgiveness, and peacemaking. Dr. Umbreit has conducted training seminars and lectures throughout the world, in Asia, Africa, Europe, the Mideast, and North and South America. Mark has been a consultant and trainer for the United States Department of Justice for the past 30 years. Dr. Umbreit also serves on the faculty of the Center for Spirituality & Healing in the Academic Health Center at the University of Minnesota, teaching courses on Peacemaking & Spirituality and Forgiveness & Healing.

As a practitioner, he facilitates peace-building circles in the community between members of diverse cultures and restorative dialogues between family survivors of homicide and the offender in their quest for healing and strength. Mark initiated the first Palestinian-Jewish dialogue group in the Minneapolis/St. Paul community, as well as a Muslim Restorative Justice Engagement Project in the Twin Cities and beyond. He is working with colleagues in Northern Ireland, Italy, Liberia, and Israel/Palestine on peace building initiatives. He has helped establish restorative justice programs in hundreds of communities, including in nearly every state of the U.S. and numerous other countries. Dr. Umbreit's multi-site and multi-national research has contributed significantly to restorative justice policy development in the U.S. and other countries, as well as providing resource materials and guidance to practitioners. Mark has also recently worked as a Senior International Consultant with the United Nations Development Program and the Ministry of Justice in Turkey to support their legislative efforts to implement victim offender mediation throughout the country.

Mark and his wife, Alexa, have for many years been dancing with the energy of severe illnesses, including cancer. They both have been trained in two energy therapies that support physical healing and spiritual development: Healing Touch, endorsed by the American Holistic Nurses Association; and, Qi ("Chi") Gong, by masters at the China Academy of Traditional Chinese Medicine, Xi Yuan Hospital, in Beijing which integrates Eastern and Western forms of medical treatment.

Made in the USA
Lexington, KY
19 March 2017